# Discovering
# HALLMARKS
# on English Silver

John Bly

F.R.S.A.

SHIRE PUBLICATIONS

# Contents

British Library Cataloguing in Publication Data: Bly, John Discovering hallmarks on English silver. - 9th ed. 1. Silver - England - Standards of fineness 2. Silverware - England - Identification I. Title 739.2'3742'0278 ISBN 0 7478 0450 8.

*The author wishes to thank Mr J. S. Forbes, Deputy Warden 1953 to 1983, and Assay Master of the Worshipful Company of Goldsmiths, London, and David W. Evans, current Deputy Warden, for their help on the chapters concerning hallmarks.*

*Published in 2000 by Shire Publications Ltd, Cromwell House, Church Street, Princes Risborough, Buckinghamshire HP27 9AA, UK.*
*Copyright © 1968, 1986, 1997 and 2000 by John Bly. First published 1968; reprinted 1969, 1970, 1971. Second edition 1974, reprinted 1976. Third edition 1978. Fourth edition 1979. Fifth edition 1981. Sixth edition 1983. Seventh edition 1986, reprinted 1988, 1992, 1993. Eighth edition 1997. Ninth edition 2000. Number 38 in the Discovering series. ISBN 0 7478 0450 8.*

Printed in Great Britain by CIT Printing Services Ltd, Press Buildings, Merlins Bridge, Haverfordwest, Pembrokeshire SA61 1XF.

# 1
# The development of hallmarks

Discovering hallmarks on English silver and learning to read them can give us an immediate knowledge of the quality, date, place of assay and thereby the approximate locality of manufacture and the maker of the piece of silver being examined, a direct and very clear link with our economic, political and domestic history. The term 'hallmark' was first used to describe the mark applied at the headquarters of the Goldsmiths' Company on articles of silver sent there to be tested to ensure that the correct standard of silver had been used in the manufacture. More recently, however, it has become generally accepted that 'hallmark' can be used as a term to describe all four or five marks on gold and silver which have been obligatory in England since the late seventeenth century.

Hallmarks were intended to show that certain legal obligations had been fulfilled and so a purchaser might buy with the assurance of a guarantee that the quality of his acquisition was correct by the standards laid down by law and, in the event of fraud, the persons responsible for making and testing the silver could be traced and punished. Hallmarks were never intended as a guide for future collectors, for until the last half of the nineteenth century there were few collectors of antique silver, certainly when compared with the nationwide hobby silver collecting has now become. Prior to the 1850s silver tended to be regarded as a commodity which could be put to immediate monetary as well as domestic use, because wrought plate (the name given to all manufactured silver articles) was the same standard metal as the coin of the realm. Before going into more detail on the marks themselves, it is necessary to realise how old their story is, and how very different life in England was in earlier times.

During the twelfth and thirteenth centuries personal fortunes were quickly gained and lost and, unlike today, complete families were inclined to move, settle down and then move on again to another part of the land. The furniture and chattels of the mobile household were therefore basic and strictly utilitarian, wealth being displayed largely by the amount of silver utensils in use and on show. There were no stocks, shares or bonds for the average man to invest in, so any surplus coinage was melted down (there was no paper money) and the silver or gold fashioned into wrought plate. Basins, ewers, drinking vessels and platters and, most important of all at that time, a standing salt were typical of the items made. On the other hand when times were hard, and cash short, the obvious solution was to take any dispensable wrought plate to a coiner and have it melted down and made into money. This worked well providing that the original silversmith had not indulged in the highly lucrative practice of adding too much copper to too little silver when the last 'money to wrought plate' transaction had occurred. House fires were frequent, and it can be imagined that large amounts of wrought plate were melted in this way, but they were, or should have been, still worth their weight in metal.

Apart from having the family plate refashioned to the current style – fashion changed then as now, albeit not so rapidly – these are just two of many reasons why a man of some substance might have discovered fraudulent manufacture of silver.

## King John and the Easterling smiths

Apparently the first monarch in England to appreciate the need for some sort of order and conformity in the manufacture of silverware was King John (reigned 1199-1216). He summoned from Germany a number of silversmiths to come to England and assist the English smiths in reducing silver to a 'fineness'. Pure silver is too soft to be 'worked' well and of too soft a composition to be durable and so it is melted and mixed with a harder base metal. This melting and mixing was called 'alloying' but recently the word alloy has become used to describe the base metal used in the mixture. The alloy for silver is copper, which has no effect on its colour. The work of the German smiths was primarily for the coin of the realm, but as wrought plate was to be of the same standard, their employment had a twofold objective. The amount of silver to alloy decided upon was 92.5% fine (pure) silver to 7.5% alloy, which proportions have remained the same (officially) from the twelfth century to the present day with the exception of a short break, 1697-1720.

The German smiths were called Easterlings by the English because they came from Germany which is to the east. This nickname was quickly and generally adopted, for early manuscripts of the time describe contemporary silver and gold coins as 'Easterlings' and later 'Esterlings'.

As can be seen, through the ages the second letter of this name was dropped and later still the first letter was also lost, so silver of good quality became known as Sterling. Long since, this name has described anything of good character and quality.

## The Standard and the early English silversmiths

Although a standard for silver had been set, it was difficult for a dishonest journeying silversmith to resist the temptation of mixing a little more alloy and a little less silver than officially required. While the wrought plate was in use, this was undetectable, but when taken for melting it could be found that the original, say, £100 worth of coin, made into twenty cups, when melted back for coin might be found to be made of only £80 worth of correct standard coin, the original smith having pocketed £20 for himself. This became in greater and lesser degrees so much a general practice that in the year 1238 an order was proclaimed by King Henry III that the Mayor and Aldermen of London should appoint six of the most reputable goldsmiths of the city to 'superintend the craft' and severely punish any smith discovered using dishonest practices.

One of the earliest records of English silversmiths in any organised body is in 1180, when an association or guild of goldsmiths (both silver and goldsmiths are referred to under this title) was fined for being irregularly established, i.e. without licence of the king, but it can be assumed that there had been a 'craft' or 'mystery' of goldsmiths for several centuries prior to that date.

Little is heard of the work of the Guild of Goldsmiths for some years but we do know that they were strong in numbers, for in 1267 it is recorded that five hundred members of the Guild of Goldsmiths and an equal number of 'Taylors' engaged in a pitched battle through the streets of London. Many were killed and their bodies thrown into the Thames, and so our silversmiths managed to make their presence known in one way or another. But fighting or not, the practice of dishonest silver manufacture apparently continued, for however enthusiastically the wardens of the Guild tried to do their job it was difficult to ensure a guaranteed standard without any tangible legislation. So in the year 1300 a statute of King Edward I provided that no ware of gold or silver should be sold until it had been taken to the headquarters of the guardians of the craft and there tested. Then, if approved, the article was to be struck with a mark as a guarantee of quality.

## The King's Mark

The mark adopted was one depicting the head of a lion, but as its use was symbolic and in early French (a popular language among the upper classes) the heraldic term describing a lion's head was 'leopart', it has since become known as the Leopard's Head. At this time the headquarters of all Guilds of Goldsmiths was still in London, and so the King's mark or Leopard's Head was soon to become recognised as the London town mark, but for the majority of the fourteenth and fifteenth centuries it was essentially a guarantee. Now although this helped considerably, it did not eliminate dishonest practice among a large number of smiths and so for the protection of both the honest smith and his client, and the exposure of the unethical silversmith, a second mark was added.

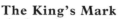

## The Maker's Mark

In 1363 a statute of King Edward III provided that every goldsmith 'should have a mark by himself' for which he should answer, to be struck beside the King's mark. Before any plate was melted a note was made of the smith's mark and then if the silver was found to be substandard the maker could be traced and held responsible.

The earliest examples of maker's marks took the form of an emblem connected with the maker's name or the sign of the shop where he worked. If, say, his name was Bell, then a punch with the design of a bell was used. If he either worked with or sold his product through a leather worker, whose shop sign would be a model of his wares or a 'play' on his name, then a leather jug might have been his mark. One existing example of this was Sir Thomas Gresham (1519-79), whose premises in Lombard Street, London, bore the sign of a grasshopper. The reason for a design rather than initials for the maker's mark was because very few people could read and so letters were of little use. By the beginning of the seventeenth century, however, it was general practice to use the first two letters of the maker's surname or his initials.

The money that could be made by selling substandard silver was still sufficient to make it worthwhile even with the addition of the compulsory maker's mark, which obviously greatly increased the risk of being caught and punished. One such smith during the fourteenth century was fined a full pipe of wine and 12 pence a week for a year, which was paid to a poor member of the Guild – a heavy fine indeed in fourteenth-century England. A great deal of the responsibility for the amount of substandard silver being sold and later discovered was certainly that of the warden whose job it was to test the silver, and during the fifteenth century it became increasingly necessary to provide some further legislation in this respect. In the year 1478 under a statute of King Edward IV a new mark was added.

## The Assay Mark or Date Letter

The operation of testing the silver was called the Assay, after the Old French *assai* meaning examination. Under a statute of 1478 the Goldsmiths' Company was made liable to a fine if it marked any substandard silver. In order to identify the assayer responsible it introduced an additional mark known as the Assay Mark. This mark was applied next to the Leopard's Head and Maker's mark and changed every year with the change of wardens. Any more symbols would make the markings too complex to read and so they used the letters of the alphabet. The London Goldsmiths' Guild decided to use the first twenty letters of the alphabet excluding J. When the letters were exhausted, the 'type' of the letter or the shape of the shield or background was changed and the alphabet started again.

By this time legislation provided for assay offices at York, Newcastle, Lincoln, Norwich, Bristol, Salisbury and Coventry although it is only at York, Newcastle and Norwich that it is certain plate was ever assayed. All of these offices were obliged to use the alphabet as Touch Warden's marks but they did not necessarily adopt the same cycle of letters as London. As early as 1378, King Richard II had given 'powers of touch' to all mayors of cities and boroughs with the help of the master of the local mint 'if there be such'. This was done to ensure that all wrought plate should, before being sold, be tested and struck in the proper manner wherever in England it might be made. At the time this seemed a logical and well-meaning idea, for to expect a silversmith in York to travel all the way to London just to have his wares stamped was too much. Not only would the journey have taken a considerable time, it was also extremely hazardous. Highway robbers could make easy money from a travelling smith.

On further reflection, however, the idea of giving local dignitaries these powers of touch was not such a good one. Mayors and other officials were elected, as now, by their local population, and if this consisted of a fair number of goldsmiths then the whole scheme was open to a certain amount of corruption. So in 1423, the Regency Council ordered special offices to be set up at the above mentioned towns, and 'to have divers touches'. In other words, each town was to comply with the legally required number of marks but the King's mark or Leopard's Head could be varied slightly in order to tell in which part of the country a particular piece of silver was made. For instance the earliest recorded mark on York silver was half a Leopard's Head and half a fleur de lis. The main point now is that by 1478 we have a standard mark, which was already becoming known as a town mark, a maker's mark, and a date letter (which was first mentioned as a letter of the year mark in 1560). This surely was enough of a guarantee of standard and enough of a deterrent to dishonest smiths and assay masters to allow maker, assayer, purchaser and treasury to relax. And so it would have been if, during the ensuing seventy-five years, the political and economic situation in England had not changed quite so drastically.

### The Standard Mark or Lion Passant

For many and diverse reasons over the years the coin of the realm had been gradually debased so much that in 1545, during the reign of Henry VIII, the coinage was worth approximately half its true value. But during this change, the standard of wrought plate remained the same. To prove this, a fourth mark was introduced by the Goldsmiths' Company in 1544. The mark, which was later recognised by statute, took the form of a lion in full profile as if walking to the left with its right paw raised. Called the Lion Passant, this mark soon became known as the Sterling mark and was to replace the Leopard's Head in its use as a standard mark. The Leopard's Head mark or its counterpart was now used to determine the place of manufacture, the maker's mark the maker, the annual letter the warden responsible for assay, and the Lion Passant the standard of the silver, thus satisfying all concerned with the manufacturing, legal, assaying, buying and selling aspects of silver. But not, unfortunately, for long. By 1600 England was economically on safer ground. In 1560, during the second year of her reign, Elizabeth I had restored the value of the coin. This was a bold step which worked and would have had everlasting results if we had not one hundred years later been recovering from the Civil War (1642-9). Apart from the appalling personal grief and misery which accompany any war, especially civil, this was a particularly sad one for the silver collector of today. Probably because it was England's most recent civil war it is thought all the more important. It was not long but it was severe, and many tons of wrought silver were melted down to pay for it. When, after the war, silversmiths were commissioned to replace the salts, platters, basins and other items that had been melted down for the war, there was naturally a shortage of silver.

This, coupled with the fact that there was with the restoration of the monarchy a coincidental rise in European trade, brings us to the next important point in our story. Here again it is necessary to review briefly the domestic economic situation in order to understand fully the need for further legislation.

### Coin clippers and the new Sterling Standard

Until the reign of Charles II English coinage was all hand-made. It was stamped by hammer and the edges cut with shears. This provided everyone, whatever their motives, with ample opportunity to make their own money. Whenever dealing with cash transactions (as against credit or transfer of chattels) the easiest thing was to clip a small piece off the edge of each coin before passing them on. Before long enough clippings could be collected, melted down and, with a fake die and stamp, minted into money. Although this had been going on for many years, and was already an offence punishable by branding or death, the demand for silver after the Civil War made coin clipping more tempting. For instead of trying to forge money with the melted down clippings, it was now possible to take them to a silversmith who would pay a handsome price, certainly as high as coin value, and in some cases a little above. This became such a popular and lucrative practice that hundreds of men and women were dragged up Holborn Hill and hanged. One 'clipper' offered £6000 for a pardon – an enormous sum. So, under the direction of Charles II, a mill worked by horses was established at the Tower of London.

The coins made at the mill were perfectly circular and an inscription or legend was engraved around the edge, so making illegal coining virtually impossible, but the new milled coins and the old hand-made coins were in circulation together. The result was that the new coins that came into general circulation were immediately hidden away. No-one would pay a new five shilling piece with five shillings worth of silver content for goods which could be bought with an old five shilling piece with say three shillings worth of silver content while clipping an extra bit off the edge for good measure. Because of the increased amount of coinage in circulation, clipping continued almost as a normal part of life. The government had to act quickly. An attempt was made to call in the old coinage and 4th May 1697 was declared as the last day. Ten furnaces had been erected behind the Treasury, which was then situated in Whitehall between the Banqueting House and the river. For several weeks, large piles of clipped and unrecognisable coins were collected, melted and made into ingots. In one instance it was recorded that over £52,000 worth (face value) of coins was paid in and, when melted, was worth little over half. However, the old coinage was eventually finished with, but not without several nasty scenes during 2nd, 3rd and 4th May 1697 when guards had to be called to quell the vast crowds of people who had hung on to their old savings until the last minute. This did not prove the complete answer, for the issue of new coinage was terribly slow. Rich and poor alike were forced to live on credit and the heavy demand for silver continued.

The next step was to eliminate one of the major reasons for the demand. In the year 1697, the standard of wrought plate was raised from 92.5% fine silver to 95.84%. Melted coin was no longer of use to the honest silversmith. This standard of silver was known as New Sterling and/or (because it was denoted with a stamp showing the figure of Britannia) the Britannia Standard. The mark was not an additional one. It was used instead of the Lion Passant, and in conjunction with another new mark, the Lion's Head Erased. This was the picture of the lion's head in profile facing the left with the effect of having been torn from the body or 'erased'. On London silver, the Lion's Head Erased replaced the Leopard's Head mark but in other assay offices it was used as well as the town mark. The new standard silver, however, proved unpopular with some silversmiths. They complained that it was too soft to work well, and as a commercial proposition it was unsuccessful. But by 1720 the economic situation had improved sufficiently for the government to agree to restore legislation of the old Sterling Standard. The Britannia Standard was not banned but was left as an option for silversmith or client to choose according to supply or requirements. So from 1720 to the present day it has been possible to have silver made of the Sterling Standard (92.5% fine silver) or the Britannia Standard (95.84% fine silver). The beginning of the eighteenth century saw the hallmarking system on wrought silver in the form we recognise it today, and so it was to remain until 1784, when the last significant change took place.

### The Sovereign's Head Mark

Silver had for many years been an ideal medium for the imposition of an extra tax for short periods, bringing additional revenue for the government. In 1784, when a new tax was put on silver, a fifth mark was added to signify that the tax had been paid. The mark was that of the King's Head in profile and the first example was George III. The collection of the duty money was the job of the Commissioners of Stamps (soon to become 'of Inland Revenue') who were assisted by the assay offices. The duty imposed, however, soon became heavier, and by the beginning of the nineteenth century (c.1815) the tax was as high as 6 pence an ounce. Inevitably this encouraged counterfeiting of the duty mark. So much, in fact, that in 1815 it was made a capital offence. The duty, and the stamp denoting the head of the reigning monarch, were enforced until the year 1890 when the tax was abolished and the mark became obsolete. So for 106 years we had an additional mark an all wrought silver (except very small articles such as jewellery mountings) which, because of its design, was known as the sovereign's head mark. It was introduced on 1st December 1784 and during the calendar year of 1785 took on a unique form for one twelvemonth only – the King's Head Intaglio. Most marks of any type are struck with a stamp which has the pattern worked into the surface, thus making the surface of the design on the metal struck convex or 'coming out' towards the viewer. Intaglio is the reverse. The date letter changed in May and so for the silversmiths' year of 1785 the profile of the King's Head was, when stamped, concave or 'going in' below the surface of the background of the stamp. The date letter or touch warden's mark for this year was a small K and the Intaglio King's Head here is a useful guide to beginners when studying silver, for the date letter for 1825 is almost identical, but can be differentiated by the King's Head mark which is of normal design. Although there are no more significant alterations in the marking of silver, another change in design should be remembered as a basic guide.

## The Leopard's Head Crowned

The Leopard's Head mark since its first innovation has had many minor alterations in style, such as with or without whiskers and changes in the shape of the shield. But the main alteration came in 1478, the year that the Date Letter was introduced, with the addition of a crown over the head of the leopard. In 1729 two pearls were added to the crown but otherwise the mark remained basically the same until 1821 when the crown was taken off for the last time. This is of particular significance to us today because the London date letters for the cycle 1776 to 1796 are, as stated earlier, almost identical with those from 1821 to 1836 and the uncrowned Leopard's Head denotes the difference between them.

The Hallmarking Act of 1973 repealed all earlier statutes and consolidated the hallmarking requirements in one Act. One change brought about by the new legislation was that all four assay offices – London, Birmingham, Sheffield and Edinburgh –were to use the same date letter, which changes on the 1st January each year.

By now we have seen how it is possible to look at any piece of English silver and tell from the marks the quality of metal used, who made it, where it was made and assayed, and when.

## The assay

The assay itself is interesting in its own right. Basically the procedure was that when an article of silver was sent for testing, it was scraped with a burin or graving tool and the resulting slivers of metal, called bohrils or diets, were then tested. The earliest method of testing was by 'touch'. The metal to be tested was rubbed on to a black, fine-grained stone such as slate and then compared with the rubbings of pure gold or pure silver. This worked reliably only with gold and was abandoned for silver assaying at a very early period. It was superseded by the fire assay method or cupellation. The scrapings are wrapped in lead foil, and placed on a cupel in a furnace (or fire). It is a refining process resulting in a blob of pure silver. Modern instrumental methods are now used for silver, but fire assay is still used for gold due to its accuracy. The name diet when applied to scrapings or bohrils comes from the early Latin *dieta* meaning day. Assaying was not done at just any time, but on certain periodically appointed days. These became known as diet days and the bohrils themselves as diets.

## Commemorative marks

During the twentieth century, there have been additional commemorative marks.

Silver Jubilee 1935   Coronation 1953   Silver Jubilee 1977   Millennium Mark

 **Hallmarks from 1999**

United Kingdom hallmarks changed on 1st January 1999. The sponsor's mark, assay office mark and fineness mark remain compulsory, the latter appearing as numbers 800, 925, 958 and 999. The year date letter is voluntary, as are the traditional symbols for 925 (lion passant) and 958 (Britannia). Unhallmarked silver of at least 800 quality can be described as silver if made before 1920.

Hallmarks and finenesses from certain other hallmarking countries in the European Economic Area are permitted. This is in addition to the International Convention Hallmark, which consists of a sponsor's mark, assay office mark, fineness mark and a Common Control Mark on 800 and 925 silver (as illustrated above).

# 2
# Domestic silver and church plate

The dining room of the average well-to-do family in the twelfth century was very different from that of today. Most houses consisted basically of one large room with various small annexes, kitchens, etc., and had very little furniture. The construction was generally like that of a large barn with stone walls and a very high ceiling and roof. The fire was in the middle of the room without a chimney, the smoke just drifting up to the roof and escaping where it could. The dining table was long and narrow and placed against one wall. When in use the table was moved out into the room to allow the master and lady of the house and guests to sit facing the fire and use the wall behind them for support. There were nearly always guests of some sort, for any man of means had a chaplain and clerks, perhaps a travelling monk might call, or a visiting baron or royal official, and of course the remaining members of the household. There were as yet no forks for use at table. Instead, jugs and basins holding water were used for washing hands during a meal. These jugs, basins, platters and the drinking vessels were made of earthenware, pewter or silver, but the true sign of prosperity was the salt cellar which stood on the table in front of the master of the house. He sat at the exact centre with his wife or lady on his left and the members of his household on her left. On his right sat the guests. Very carefully they were placed in order of wealth and/or merit from the most important on his immediate right down to the least important and probably unknown traveller at the end. This placing was a most important part of table etiquette and was recognised as sitting 'in order of the salt'. Two of our present-day phrases are derived from this: 'worth his salt', and 'right-hand man'.

Apart from the shape and style of an article of silver, the piece itself can give a good clue as to whether or not it is contemporary with the hallmarks or of the period it should be. Some provincially made silver, although assayed in London, can be several years behind the latest styles. This might also occur when silver was made to match existing plate. Here are one or two general guide lines to follow. There were no tea kettles, tea caddies or teapots before the latter part of the seventeenth century because until that period there was no large-scale tea drinking in England. Until changes in social etiquette demanded their introduction in the mid eighteenth century, there were no decanter stands or wine labels. There are comparatively few examples of the big ewers and basins used for washing hands at table after the beginning of the eighteenth century because the innovation of the table fork dispensed with the need for them. Spoons, however, are our most important domestic utensils in connection with hallmarks. Some of the earliest recorded marks are on spoons and, having been made in vast quantities since earliest times, there is always the chance of finding a rare and early specimen 'in the attic'.

Although the standing salt cellar was still important at table, by the end of the seventeenth century it was more of a symbol, and it disappeared during the early eighteenth century. By this time it was common practice for each person to have a portion of salt next to his plate. This was in a small individual salt cellar, known as a trencher salt. Trencher salts went out of fashion during the early eighteenth century in favour of sets of salt cellars and cruet frames. The earliest of these frames had all silver casters, but cruets with finely cut glass bottles with silver mountings were popular by the middle of the eighteenth century. While the trencher salt as such had gone, the individual small salt cellar remained, but it is unusual now to find more than eight in a set.

Tankards are among the more popular items for collectors today. Apart from their utility value, they reflect the changing styles and fashions in their shape and decoration as well as any other single domestic article. The name tankard originally meant any large vessel of wood bound with hoops of brass or other metal, and which held three or more gallons of liquid. It was not used to describe drinking vessels until the sixteenth century. Before then secular cups were called beakers. The earliest type of cup had no handle; it had straight sides and a flat base. In the fourteenth century, they were called bikers, then later bekers, which changed again to beakers. We now use the word beaker to describe a handleless straight-sided cup, and tankard to describe a vessel of any shape with one handle and a lid. The open-topped pint pot is called a mug, although this particular type is rare before the middle of the seventeenth century.

Some of the finest early silver is in England's churches.

Every church has some and if arrangements are made with the local church authority – who are extremely helpful – it may be possible to see some wonderful silver and study the craftsmanship and read the hallmarks. It is always preferable to make an appointment to see any church plate because it is usually kept in the local bank, but it is certainly well worth the trouble.

Prior to the Reformation the churches had for the celebration of the Holy Sacrament a chalice, which is a tall cup on a thin stem with a spread circular base; a paten, which is like a small plate with a circular base; two ewers for wine and water; and the pyx, which is the box in which the Host is kept. The number of sacred vessels and other articles such as candlesticks, croziers, bells and processional crosses depended on the size and wealth of the particular church.

Although the Reformation began as a political change and under Henry VIII was concerned mainly with the monasteries, during the reign of Edward VI (1547-1553) it became almost fanatically religious, and irreparable damage was done in England's churches. Brasses were dug out and destroyed, manuscripts were burnt, figures and tombs were defaced and windows smashed. But most important to the student of early silver, all ecclesiastical plate was sorted through and everything but the essential items was confiscated. Rather than have this happen many church authorities melted down the silver for coinage which could be hidden and used for other purposes. Ecclesiastical pre-Reformation silver is therefore rare. However, as the strict laws governing the methods of worship were gradually relaxed, church plate became more plentiful. The quality of manufacture and the decoration of all church plate has always been of the very highest standard. This continued at times when, because of either economic reasons or pure fashion, domestic silver was of the simplest and most basic design.

# 3
# Collecting silver

The outline plan for starting a collection need never be too strict. Often a collection started in one particular field has changed as the collection grew, until the end result, if there ever is an end result for a keen collector, has been an entirely different sort of collection to the one originally envisaged. Many people are perhaps overawed by the thought of having to collect one type of silver article or one particular maker and find after they have committed themselves that they wish they had started to collect something else. If the collection is formed with good advice the changeover need not result in financial disadvantage, but it is preferable to start without too firm intentions as to the future of the collection.

One heading which encompasses possibly the largest variety of different types of utensil is that of silver-mounted objects. From the earliest times various materials have been mounted with silver or gold. The insertion of semi-precious stones is one of the earliest forms of enrichment. For domestic and utility items the collector need not be in awe of having to collect something from the thirteenth and fourteenth centuries for ivory, wood and horn were all mounted with silver throughout the eighteenth and nineteenth centuries. Under this heading come glass snuff bottles with silver caps, travelling cutlery sets and picnic sets (where a cup has a velvet-lined wooden case into which slot the folding knife, fork and spoon), shaving sets of gentlemen's toilet services, cruet sets and innumerable other items. Silver-mounted cups are an ideal choice; among the illustrations are two beakers made of horn. The lip of each bears a rim of silver engraved with bright cut decoration in the Classical style and each is fully hallmarked.

Another type of cup found dating from medieval times is the silver-mounted coconut cup. While these date from the early sixteenth century such examples are, of course, extremely rare and it is those produced during the eighteenth and nineteenth centuries that are most commonly found today. Generally speaking, the fashion for coconut cups, essentially drinking vessels, sometimes lidded and thought to have magical powers, declined during the late sixteenth century, although occasional examples from the next two hundred years still appear on the market from time to time. The fashion revived during 1755-75, presumably because of their Gothic associations.

Even earlier in its associations and origins is the drinking bowl known as the mazer. This is a circular turned wood bowl with silver-mounted rim usually bearing a silver disc known as a 'print' on the inside at the centre of the bowl. The word mazer is said to be derived from the German *mase* meaning spot and alludes to the fact that the turned wood bowls were made from that part of the maple tree where one branch joins another. Obviously this is extremely hard and would be more resistant to liquid than the softer wood of the branch. Knowledge of such silver-mounted objects can lead into the study of treen, another subject entirely. Alternatively the mounts themselves can be sought for collection and the prints from mazers are an example. These are generally $2^1/2$ to $3^1/2$ inches (64-90 mm) in diameter, embossed in bas-relief with mythological or allegorical scenes and subjects within a border pierced regularly with small holes. At first glance a mazer print appears to be part of a costume, for the closeness of the holes would lead one to assume that the print was stitched to a part of a dress or habit. The holes were to take the small-headed pins that fastened the print to the bottom of the bowl. The print itself, like so many decorative features, was undoubtedly first used as a practical measure, serving to cover the holes left by the lathe as well as to prevent leakage through what might be a weakened part of the wood. It was soon realised that this practical measure could be turned into a decorative feature.

The price of any particular piece of antique silver is governed by many things. The current market value or scrap price has some effect, although the weight is considered more to discover whether or not extensive alterations have occurred. Silver is weighed in Troy ounces and pennyweights, and most silver has its weight very lightly scratched on the underside at the time of manufacture. This scratchweight, as it is known, was done freehand with a very sharp pointed instrument, and in many cases has been worn away through the years. When this is visible, however, it is possible by weighing to discover if any superstructure has been added or any large parts, such as inscriptions and plates bearing coats of arms, have been polished off or taken away. (Allow a small discrepancy for normal cleaning and general use.) The age is very important but not overriding. Pre-eighteenth-century silver has for many years been expensive, but only recently has all George I (1714-27) silver been making nearer its true value. Tea kettles and urns of the mid eighteenth century are still underpriced compared with teapots, coffee pots and hot water jugs of the same date. As more and more people continue to collect silver the price rises, and the period when articles form cabinet collections instead of utility collections gets later and later. Whereas a George I pen tray might well have been used on a desk, it is now more likely to be the centrepiece in a cabinet and no more than carefully washed once a fortnight. Therefore the 'age price' is governed in turn by the saleability of the individual item unless it is of an early period when scarcity and therefore high price make it impractical to use. The general condition of the article itself and the condition of the marks it bears are also important factors, but not, in some cases, all-important. These and the other guiding rules can be waived when a piece of silver bears the mark of certain famous makers.

Without dwelling on the financial aspects of collecting, it is worth remembering that apart from the Art Nouveau, Arts and Crafts and Art Deco styles of silver produced from about 1890 to 1920 there was also a considerable amount of very fine quality reproduction silver, described in contemporary catalogues as Queen Anne or Georgian style. The Queen Anne was for the most part true to its original counterpart and tea and coffee services were made of octagonal pear-shape form, generally of appropriately heavy gauge metal. The sizes of the tea and coffee services vary greatly and attractive collections can be formed of such pieces as they are both decorative and useful. The Georgian pattern is generally less true in its reproduction. The shapes vary in plan from rectangular to oval, the former generally squat baluster, the latter slightly tapered; both have the semi-lobing so popular during the 1810-30 period. Here again the quest for the finest quality and most pleasing shape creates sufficient interest to form the basis for a collection and, once started, there is no telling what direction the collection will take and where, if ever, it may end.

# 4
# Fakes and alterations

Despite the rigorously applied hallmarking laws on English silver, the collector today should be aware of the existence of certain types of spurious plate. All items of antique English wrought plate, with the exception of very small pieces, should bear the requisite hallmarks. (In the context of this chapter the word antique should be understood to mean silver made during the seventeenth, eighteenth and early nineteenth centuries.) For numerous and varied reasons examples of unmarked antique plate continue to appear. After 1st January 1975 (in accordance with the Hallmarking Act 1973) such pieces could be sold as silver if they were made before 1900 and had not been altered. However, if an article has undergone such alteration, for even the most innocent of reasons, as to change its essential character it may not be legally sold until the alteration has been regularised by an assay office. The point of an innocent reason for alteration is made to draw to the reader's attention the essential difference between alteration for utility or aesthetic reasons and alteration effected for purely financial reward. As it was not until the latter part of the nineteenth century that any appreciable interest in antique silver became apparent it is obvious that altered pieces and most items of fake silver manufactured for pecuniary gain stem from that period. During the earlier periods an article may have been altered because the owner could not afford the cost of complete remaking. During the nineteenth century there was the additional incentive of 'bringing up to date' inherited plain silver by embossing it with the floral and foliate designs so popular during the William IV and Victorian periods. For example, countless eighteenth-century tankards were converted into jugs during the 1850s by having a spout added opposite the handle and by having the baluster body and domed lid embossed in a floral design, often of the highest quality. If the jug were to contain hot liquid the handle was often cut and insulated with two ivory washers. As long as all additional pieces to an item of silver are hallmarked at the time of construction, the item will comply with the law.

What is not acceptable is any form of forged hallmark or the insertion of hallmarks from one piece into another, as when the marks on the back of an antique spoon are let into the neck of a new coffee pot, the solder line often being disguised with repoussé decoration. Such a line may or may not be visible by frosting the surface, an effect commonly achieved by breathing on the piece of silver. (Metal is generally colder than breath and silver solder and any other imperfection become immediately more apparent through the resulting condensation.) If this experiment shows any further reason for suspicion expert advice should be sought.

Another type of silver which may be encountered is the 'duty dodger'. The amount of tax payable was determined by the weight of the article; thus when the tax became prohibitively high (it is recorded in 1804 at one shilling and three pence per ounce) there was great temptation for a silversmith constructing a large piece of silver to find a convenient place to insert a small piece of silver, properly assayed and hallmarked, in order to evade the duty on the majority of silver used in the manufacture of the article. Sale of pieces with forged or transposed hallmarks is illegal until they have been regularised by an assay office. According to the Hallmarking Act 1973, if the hallmarks were struck on an article or transposed into it before 1854 the assay office will cancel them without actually obliterating them.

While it is preferable for a collector to seek a piece without blemish or fault of any kind it is inevitable that articles with a minor repair, removed dent or re-engraving will continue to appear. There are, however, degrees of seriousness regarding later engraving. Much domestic plate made in the eighteenth and early nineteenth centuries was specifically commissioned for a particular family with the appropriate coat of arms, crest or suitable presentation inscription being engraved as part of the commission at the time. The busy silversmith took care to produce surplus items in the classification which he knew to be in constant demand, i.e. small waiters, coffee pots, beer tankards and other utility items, some of which were sold without any engraving. Such pieces have always held considerable interest for the collector as they can be said to be in pristine condition; the exception to this is when the crest, coat of arms or presentation inscription belongs or alludes to personages of importance or high standing, a member of any royal family, or an event of national significance. However, during the 1890s, the early 1900s, the period between the two world wars and immediately following the Second World War, it was found that a crest or presentation inscription, contemporary or later, detracted from the commercial value of an article of silver. It was a regrettable but common practice to have such engraving erased by removing a layer of silver to the depth of the engraving. If a subsequent owner then required a further crest or inscription to be engraved the silver became even thinner. After the first erasing it was common practice to hammer the silver from below to present a fresh and flush surface on which to re-engrave. Another removal may still have been possible but it is unlikely that the silver was of sufficient gauge to allow a third, in which event the upper surface to be engraved was beaten back again and the resulting dip filled. To disguise or camouflage any difference in colour the outer surface was often electroplated. In the photographs of the late Rococo salver the indentation caused by upward beating can be clearly seen; so too can the effects of the reverse process. Such an item is at this stage utterly spurious. To establish at a preliminary investigation whether or not an engraving has been removed from the surface of a piece of silver the area under suspicion should be viewed obliquely, when an irregular dip may become apparent. A recent erasing will be spotted by the difference in colour of the patina or surface 'skin', the effect created by countless tiny scratches caused by daily use, handling and washing during the life of the article. If neither of these visual tests proves conclusive then gentle pressure between finger and thumb placed on opposite sides of the silver will establish the gauge of the metal and if the finger and thumb are then moved to the suspect area a noticeable difference will be felt.

Goldsmiths Hall offers a further service in the form of the Antique Plate Committee, which determines the authenticity of any suspect item presented for adjudication. Pieces which may have been altered in character and use by the addition or removal of silver, an item bearing transposed hallmarks or an outright fake are among the items investigated. Altered pieces may be hallmarked anew but the other categories will be broken up as they are illegal. This unique committee is further testimony to the integrity with which the sale of British silver is controlled.

# 5
# *Famous makers*

## Paul de Lamerie

Paul de Lamerie was entered in the London Guild of Gold-smiths in 1712. Although many contemporaries equalled his skill he is the most popular early eighteenth-century silversmith today. Any piece of silver of the period 1712 to *c*.1750 and bearing his mark will make a far higher price on the open market than a similar piece of the same date made by anyone else. Lamerie was a Huguenot and was commissioned by royalty, by City halls and by the nobility in general to make elaborate and highly decorative silver to the Rococo style. His work was not confined to this type, however, for during his life he produced many articles of strictly utility and functional value, and it is in these albeit charming pieces that one can compare the amazing price variation with those of his contemporaries.

Lamerie's mark was first a capital LA with a crown and mullet (small star) above and a fleur de lis below. On 17th March 1732 the letters were changed to capital PL, retaining the crown, mullet and fleur de lis. In 1739 the capital letters were changed to 'script' or long-hand capital form. The change in 1739 was in common with most other silversmiths who had been working at the time of the restoration of the old Sterling Standard in 1720. Nearly all decided to adopt new marks in that year, some using the marks they had used before 1697, others making up completely new ones. It was therefore difficult to trace makers from their marks after 1720; so much so that in 1739 an Act was passed which stated, among other things, that all old makers' marks were to be destroyed and new ones made, each smith using the initial letters of his Christian name and surname.

## Hester Bateman

Hester Bateman, whose mark is a simple HB in script, is another maker whose stamp will increase the value of a piece of silver today. Hester Bateman first introduced her mark at the Goldsmiths' Hall in 1761 and for many years was responsible for the production of fine silver, beautifully designed and wrought. She retired in 1790, the business being continued by her sons Peter and Jonathon. Their mark is a capital PB over IB. In 1791 Jonathon Bateman died and his widow Ann Bateman, nee Dowling, entered a mark with Peter Bateman, her brother-in-law. This mark was a capital PB over AB. The fourth mark of the Bateman family business is often the basis for some confusion, being the triple mark of PB over AB over WB, the mark of Peter, Ann and William Bateman. This was formed when William Bateman, son of Ann and Jonathon, joined the partnership. The mark of Peter and William Bateman, PB over WB, was introduced in 1805 following Ann's retirement.

Hester Bateman was by no means the only woman silver-smith in the eighteenth century: indeed there are records of women silversmiths from the early sixteenth century. Many deserve greater recognition than they have received. One in particular is Rebecca Emes, wife of John Emes, who following her husband's death formed a partnership with the workshop foreman in her husband's company and registered the mark RE over EB in a quatrefoil shield: Rebecca Emes and Edward Barnard.

## Eliza Godfrey

During the middle years of the eighteenth century, the most important and prolific lady silversmith was undoubtedly Eliza, widow of Benjamin Godfrey and former wife of Abraham Buteaux. The product of Eliza Godfrey's workshop was invariably of the highest quality, with much use of fine casting and chasing in conjunction with pierced fretwork of the most intricate designs in the pure Rococo and transition styles. Most examples of her work date from the 1740s following the death of her husband in 1741.

## Samuel Wood and Nathaniel Mills

Other makers who appear to have specialised in one type of article are numerous, but contrary to what might be expected, their name on such an article has little effect on the price compared with the effect of a Lamerie or a Bateman mark. Two examples are Samuel Wood – entered London 1733: mark SW – who made casters, dredgers, ewers and anything else connected with cruets and cruet frames until approximately 1773, and Nathaniel Mills – entered Birmingham 1825: mark NM later N.M. – who made snuff boxes. Although Mills was responsible for some of the finest snuff boxes made in the nine-teenth century, and his name is synonymous with quality, a good box by a little-known maker can be worth the same price.

## Paul Storr

Perhaps the most famous of early nineteenth-century silver-smiths was Paul Storr – mark P.S. A London maker, he was, like Lamerie, commissioned by royalty. His work is ornate, with extreme fineness of detail, and his castings of figures and other applied decoration are superbly drawn and executed. Unlike Lamerie, however, Storr appears to have made very little ordinary or plain silver. One contributing factor could be that Lamerie had to contend with the enforced Britannia Standard, although examples of Storr's work are made of Britannia Standard silver. Probably the main reason is that by the beginning of the nineteenth century Storr, having attained for himself the wealthiest clientele possible, left it to the many other silver-smiths to produce commercial silverware.

## Other makers

Striking a medium level, however, there are very many silversmiths of the eighteenth and nineteenth centuries whose work should merit special recognition for a continual high standard of design and execution; there are far too many to list here, but here are a few who are generally accepted as good makers, and whose work might be of interest to anyone think-ing of starting a collection.

*Peter and Jonathon Bateman* (sons of Hester Bateman) – entered 1790.
Mark $\left\{ \begin{array}{c} PB \\ IB \end{array} \right\}$

*Peter and Ann Bateman* (Ann married Jonathon Bateman and worked with her brother-in-law Peter after Jonathon's death) – entered *c.*1740.
Mark $\left\{ \begin{array}{c} PB \\ AB \end{array} \right\}$

*Peter, Ann and William Bateman* (Ann's son William) – entered 1800.
Mark $\left\{ \begin{array}{c} PB \\ AB \\ WB \end{array} \right\}$

*John Cafe* – entered *c.*1740. Mark I.C.
Fine candlesticks, chamber sticks, snuffers and trays.

*Ebenezer Coker* – entered 1758. Mark E.C.
Mostly trays, waiters, salvers.

*The Courtald family* – from *c.*1708.
>   Fine silver to high styled designs.

*John Crouch* – entered 1808. Mark I.C. first, later JC.
>   General larger silver.

*William Eley* – entered in partnership      Mark ⎧ WE ⎫
>   in 1808 with William Fearn and                 ⎨ WF ⎬
>   William Chawner.                              ⎩ WC ⎭

*William Eley junior and William Fearn* – registered mark in 1824.
>   Mark ⎧ WE ⎫
>        ⎩ WF ⎭
>   Best known for flatware.

*John Emes* – entered 1796. Mark curly J·E.
>   All fine silver.

*Garrard family* – from *c.*1729.
>   Fine silver engraving and jewellery.

*James Gould* – entered 1723. Mark IG with crown over.
>   Mostly taper sticks and candlesticks.

*Robert Hennell* – entered 1753. Mark RH.
>   Fine quality small silver, sweetmeat baskets, epergnes, salt
>   cellars, spoons, forks and other tableware.

*David and Robert Hennell* – entered 1768. Mark D·H with R over and H
>   below.
>   Fine small silver.

*Robert and Samuel Hennell* – entered 1802. Mark ⎧ RH ⎫
>   General fine silver.                              ⎩ SH ⎭

*Mappin and Webb* – company founded in 1810.
>   All fine quality pieces.

*Omar Ramsden and Alwyn Carr* – partnership with joint mark in 1898.
>   Mark $R^{n}$ & $C^{r}$
>   Celtic influence or art nouveau pieces.

*John Tuite* – entered *c.*1723. Mark I.T. in script, flanking a jug.
>   Important salver maker.

*Edward Wakelin* – entered 1747. Mark E.W. Old English
>   capitals. Prince of Wales plumes over.
>   Cans, caddies, tureens.

*Benjamin West* – entered 1739. Mark B W in script.
>   Fine tankards.

# 6
# *A guide to silver styles*

The formative years of the hallmarking system in England were a very long time ago and the silver made in those years is extremely rare. For the present-day collector the most interesting periods therefore begin in the sixteenth century, continuing through Commonwealth, Restoration, Britannia Standard, Rococo, Adam Classic, Renaissance, Regency and Victorian to Art Nouveau.

## Early silver

Generally speaking, the styles of wrought plate prior to the Commonwealth, 1649-60, were highly decorated and took much of their basic outline in the manner of the current designs in ecclesiastical architecture. The changes in these designs can be simplified in this manner.

The thirteenth century produced the first originally English variant of the Romanesque patterns which had existed since the Conquest in 1066, and which we have labelled 'Saxon' and 'Norman', or collectively 'Gothic'. This new style has been called 'Early English' or 'Lancet'. The fourteenth century, which included the innovation of geometric and curvilinear designs, is known as 'Decorated', and the fifteenth century 'Perpendicular'. The progress of architectural design was severely halted by the Black Death, 1348-9, and the Perpendicular style remained in use in connection with church building until the Reformation, around 1535. As the silver of these periods relied so strongly on church architecture for its outlines contemporary silver has been given the title of 'Gothic', covering the periods and styles mentioned above and dating from around 1175 to 1525. During the sixteenth century English silversmiths were freer with design, influenced not only by pre-Reformation ideas, but also by ideas from Europe. Cups were made from crystal or horn and then skilfully mounted. Precious and semi-precious stones were used as adornments on chargers (large plates), salts and cups, and finely modelled figures of birds and animals were popular Elizabethan patterns. This period – until 1603 – has been called Renaissance but is now generally known as Elizabethan.

During the reign of Charles I (1625-49) silver became gradually plainer, probably under the increasing Puritanical influence in the country as a whole. Simplicity in design and lack of adornment were universal by the mid 1650s. Commonwealth silver was strictly functional, usually heavy and without any unnecessary decoration. With the restoration of the monarchy in 1660 came a reversal of attitudes and ideas. High living and all that goes with it were popular and, in common with other furnishings, silver became highly decorative. The influence on the designs in the early years after the Restoration was Dutch. Charles II had been in exile in Europe and brought back with him several fashions that gained immediate popularity. A pattern characteristic of this type of early Restoration silver decoration is the heavy embossing of fruit, leaves, flowers and scrolls, somewhat similar to much of the embossing done by the Victorians. Some of the finest silversmiths in Europe at this time, however, were the Huguenots of France.

## The Huguenots

The name Huguenot was given to the French Protestants during the mid sixteenth century. They were strong in number and power and in 1598 the French king Henry IV introduced a law that gave his Protestant subjects considerable religious freedom and full civil rights. The charter was signed in Nantes, a city in western France, and is known as the Edict of Nantes. This caused much consternation to the French Catholics as the Protestants were a political as well as a religious threat to their power, and on 18th October 1685 the Edict of Nantes was completely revoked and the Huguenots were deprived of all civil and religious liberty. The effects of this caused large numbers of Huguenots to flee the country, many of them seeking refuge in England, which was at that time under the Protestant rule of Charles II. Luckily for England, among the Huguenots were silversmiths, and their influence on the design of silver becomes increasingly apparent towards the end of the seventeenth century. Because they were commissioned mainly by royalty, titled gentry and the very rich, their work was of heavy gauge silver and relied on delicacy of line and elegance for effect rather than on over-decoration.

As with any period of extreme, the highly decorated Restoration era was followed by a reversion to simplicity. By this time silver was being used for decoration on mirror frames, firedogs and any manner of extravagance. This type was very thin and embossed, and was made concurrently with the heavier domestic silver already mentioned. England was trading with the East Indies, and for a short time a popular motif was Chinese-style decoration, although examples of this type are rare today.

During the latter part of the seventeenth century, yet another most important change in the social habits of the English people took place through the East Indies trade – the import of tea. Because of its high price tea was confined for many years to the homes of the wealthy. However, there must have been a considerable number answering that description, for in 1700 the Joyners' Company announced that in four years their members had registered the manufacture of 6,582 tea tables, so it can be assumed that approximately the same number of teapots, tea urns, kettles, hot water jugs, cream jugs and sugar basins were made to go on the tables, and most of them in silver. By 1697 the standard of wrought plate was raised, and because of the softer material designs became generally plainer. Embossing was already *passé* and had been replaced by the 'cut-card' method of decoration. This was particularly suitable for Britannia Standard silver as the outline of the decoration was cut from a flat sheet of silver, usually the same thickness as the article being made, and then the pattern was applied straight on to the surface of the article, giving an appearance of very low relief. Another currently popular style was the hexagonal or octagonal pear shape. This was used on a large amount of domestic silverware, especially tea services, dredgers and casters. It was peculiar to the Britannia Standard period, and reproduction silver made since 1900 after this fashion is often labelled Queen Anne style. This simplicity of line and 'cut-card' work continued well into the beginning of the eighteenth century, but the relaxing of the Enforced High Standard law, and the now constant desire for change, brought a return to more ornate silver.

## Eighteenth century and Rococo

Presented with the option of using the new or old Sterling Standard silver, the freedom in choice of decoration and style was wide. Once settled, the style of most domestic plate changed little from 1720 until 1765, and the collective name for silver of this period is Rococo, although, through increasing scarcity in recent years, any articles made during the first three quarters of the eighteenth century are now carefully described as George I (1714-27), George II (1727-60) and George III (1760-1820).

The word Rococo is said to derive from the French *rocaille*, meaning rock work, and was used to describe this style because rocks and other inorganic forms were popular motifs incorporated in the decoration of the more elaborate furniture and silver of the period. The design was first popular in north-western Europe, particularly in France during the reign of Louis XIV, and it was brought to England in the early 1700s. Rococo also includes all manner of scrolls, curves, figures, drapes, festoons, chasing and embossing, in general any extravagant adornment. One outline in particular which was used by ordinary country silversmiths was the *campana* or bell shape. For jugs of all sizes, cups, dredgers and casters the design was ideal. The main body was the shape of a bell upturned, continuing down from the widest part which formed the lip to the narrowest part on a short incurving stem spreading on a circular base; a single or double curve 'C scroll' handle was added to one side for a jug or to two sides for a cup. Another shape to gain universal appeal was the baluster. This line was a simple open top curving in toward the base, out to form a belly and in again to join a squat spreading base. The baluster shape has been used for mugs and tankards since the beginning of the eighteenth century, but its possible variations made it a sound basic shape for many other articles.

## The Late Georgian period

Soon after the succession to the throne of George III the style of silver changed noticeably for the first time in forty years. The wealth of the country was spreading through the middle classes, increasing the desire of the average man to read, learn, travel and generally take advantage of the new opportunities which were springing up all over England. A great vogue for severity and elegance in design was appearing, due to increased interest in classical history, and under the guidance of the brothers Adam was to become powerful enough to make any other style quite unacceptable. The fact that silver was now within the reach of a larger proportion of the community, plus the introduction of the new neo-classic style, enabled the silversmiths to expand their businesses to fulfill the demand. The new elegant vase and urn shapes could be produced in much thinner silver than the previous Rococo style, and thereby costs could, when necessary, be kept down to accommodate the requirements of a larger clientele. The often huge, purely ornamental silver produced for the very wealthy in nearly all previous decades went out of fashion, to return in the early nineteenth century with the monumental and commemorative pieces of the Trafalgar era around 1805, and to another heyday in the Regency period. (Historically this covered the years 1811 to 1820 when the Prince of Wales ruled as Regent, but in design the term Regency can apply to anything made from 1800 to 1825.)

This period of English silver expanded in so many ways: new techniques of manufacture, the partnership of hitherto competing silversmiths, methods of marketing, all were changing. The great age of domestic silver had begun. England's wealth was such that comparatively little silver of this period was melted down for cash. Most damage was done from now on in the alteration of articles to keep them in line with current fashion. It should be made clear that while the leaders of fashion and the pieces made to their requirements can be traced to an almost exact date, fashions in general did not change overnight. Some of the most pleasing domestic silver comes from the overlapping periods when, while a silversmith was not prepared to adopt the latest style immediately, he was perhaps pleased to ease off a little on the previous fashion. Hence some of the most graceful and simple, yet definitely Rococo rather than Classic, silver was produced in the late 1760s and early 1770s. The silversmith never before had so wide a market and this freedom of design began to run wild. By the early nineteenth century there was no conformity of design. High fashion from 1800 saw many styles: Egyptian, Naval, Trafalgar, French (while England was at war with France, the French king Louis XVIII was living in exile near Aylesbury), Chinese, Indian, Regency, and Egyptian again. It was quick to change and was available to those who could afford it. The wealthy middle class, already becoming set in its ways and slow to change, had its silver made as it liked it. The styles and uses of articles of silver in the early nineteenth century were as varied and impossible to categorise as the people who commissioned their manufacture.

## The Victorian age

In 1830 the Georgian period finished with the end of George IV's ten-year reign. He was succeeded by William IV, whose period as monarch was to leave a marked influence on design. Freedom of extravagance in decoration by this time had overrun itself and already the form for the heavy bulbous styles of the future Victorian age was set. The one important shape to appear during the reign of William IV was what we know as 'melon'. More akin to a peeled orange, the usually circular shape was fluted to form segments. Most popular in tea services, the squashed circular shape was waisted and curved out at the top, the upper lip or edge being decorated with a band of cast fruit or flowers. The base was again waisted to curve out to a spreading foot which was often decorated to match the top.

The application of bands of floral decoration remained popular until the mid nineteenth century, by which time the impending Great Exhibition of 1851 and new techniques in manufacture caused changes in design. Victorian Gothic, rustic and later Classic designs were used from the 1840s on. The Gothic was a renaissance of earlier ecclesiastical designs, the most common being that of the geometric period of the fourteenth century whereby the use of circles cut within circles gave the impression, with the use of cluster columns and arches, of the puritanical and religious effect so popular with some Victorians. Unfortunately, as with nearly every renaissance, the original idea was 'improved', which usually means over-embellished. Thus Victorian Gothic design, whether in silver or in any other medium, so often appears very heavy.

The nineteenth-century love of naturalistic decoration went beyond the floral achievements of the earlier periods. The use of trees, vines and other forms of plant life had a large following in what we call Victorian rustic. This was really a renaissance and enlargement of the mid seventeenth-century fashion, but for once most of the nineteenth-century designs had enough originality to be instantly recognisable. Branches and roots of trees were used to decorate the main body of an article, but continued up to form handles and spouts, and down to form feet and stands.

## Art Nouveau

Towards the end of the nineteenth century many factors were to contribute towards a new and original art form labelled Art Nouveau. Most Art Nouveau of the 1890-1910 period can be described as movement in still life. A piece of furniture, silver, china or glass was designed to appear to be growing from the place where it stood. Theatre posters, fabrics and wallpapers of this period are among the most popular examples today of true Art Nouveau. Following the early period the fashion became immensely popular and was accepted for a short while in almost all types of merchandise and incorporated in the manufacture of all types of household goods.

The name Art Nouveau stuck, and for the next fifteen years any work made by designers already famous for their previous contributions was called Art Nouveau. A case in point is the famous partnership of silversmiths Omar Ramsden and Alwyn Carr. Their work had (almost like a trademark at first, but later much copied by competitors) the effect of being hand-beaten or planished, the resulting little indentations being left as an integral part of the surface. They also often incorporated the setting and application of semi-precious stones such as agate and quartz in the embossed designs on their work, and often wrote in pseudo-Gothic capital letters OMAR RAMSDEN AND ALWYN CARR ME FECIT somewhere on the finished article. Although they continued production well into the 1920s silver made by them is still labelled Art Nouveau, despite the fact that by this time the basic designs had begun to change. A demand for antique-style silver had grown, and with the economic crisis following the First World War (1914-18), and the accent on rebuilding rather than refurnishing, newly made silver was basically utilitarian and fairly plain. The times when the design and styles of silver reflected those of the current tastes of the population were over, because the renewed and apparently permanent interest and vogue for the antique have made taste difficult to categorise. The great age of custom-made domestic silver was over, but it has left us with a tangible part of our history.

# 7
# *Sheffield plate*

'One man there has discovered the art of plating copper with silver. I bought a pair of candlesticks for two guineas, they are quite pretty.' So wrote Horace Walpole on 1st September 1760 to Mrs Montague following his visit to Sheffield, and the man he spoke of was one Thomas Bolsover.

However, the term 'Sheffield plate' is now used to describe a method of production rather than the precise provenance of an article. Basically it refers to any item made in the same manner as silver, i.e. raised and domed, or in any other way beaten into shape from a sheet of metal comprising one or two layers of silver and a core layer of copper, and by the nineteenth century it was made in other areas as well, most notably in Birmingham.

Its invention was attributed to Bolsover, a cutler and mechanic, in the 1740s in Sheffield and its production was for some years limited to buttons and buckles and other small pieces. By the 1770s it had become apparent that this fusion of metals could be used to create any domestic article hitherto made of solid silver at a far reduced cost, and the great age of Sheffield plate began.

Its heyday was in the period 1790-1830 and from its conception until its demise many changes were made in the methods of manufacture and the production of decorative ornamentation, and recognition of these can today give us reasonably accurate guides to dating.

The first and most important feature to remember is that as the layered metal was forced into its new shape the edges tended to fray. To alleviate this and to add some strength to the finished edge, the lip was cut at an angle of approximately 45 degrees, leaving the outer skin of silver extending beyond the underlying copper. This extended edge was then rolled over to create a firm joint and the clearly evident 'rolled-over edge'.

As Sheffield plate closely followed the changes in styles and decoration, the onset of the Classical period enabled its fashionable manufacture with considerable ease, because the simple vase shapes with sweeping spouts and handles were ideally suited to the new material in contrast to the Baroque and

Rococo shapes that had held sway for the previous fifty years and which by their very nature required time-consuming and therefore expensive production.

In the early nineteenth century foliate and shell borders became fashionable and by the 1820s these were stamped out and applied, having first been lead-filled. Over-zealous cleaning in the Victorian period has often been responsible for wearing away the silver to expose the lead interior.

By the 1830s, however, experiments were being carried out on the potential of electrolysis, and the firm of Elkington developed a method whereby an item made of copper was placed inside a vat together with an ingot of pure silver and an electric current was passed therein. The silver transposed itself on to the copper and electroplate was born.

One important difference between the two finished articles is that Sheffield plate uses Sterling silver while electroplate employs pure silver. There is a difference in colour to the tutored eye.

By the 1850s white metal or nickel had become a popular alternative to copper and EPNS (electroplated nickel silver) became part of the silver industry. Any base metal could be used in the new process with Britannia metal (EPBM) and brass being among the most popular. When the revival of earlier styles appeared in the 1890s it is the use of either of these metals that will distinguish the later copy from the eighteenth-century original.

When any item made of silver plate is cleaned too harshly, the underground material will show through. On copper this is called a 'bleed'. It is an ongoing problem to know whether or not to replate an item which is thus worn and it is largely a matter of personal taste. As a general guide it is better to leave old period Sheffield plate well alone.

No legally enforced system of identification similar to the hallmarks on Sterling silver was applied to Sheffield plate. Early pieces were rarely marked at all. However, by the end of the eighteenth century various manufacturers had adopted the practice of stamping their wares to such a degree that there was concern that they might be mistaken for those of their Sterling silver counterparts. Careful scrutiny and a little practice will quickly enable the enthusiast to recognise the difference, for in most cases the maker's name in full is made to fit into one of the tiny rectangular marks. Throughout the nineteenth century symbols were popular, sometimes an allusion to a maker's name, sometimes in addition to and later in conjunction with EPNS and EPBM. 'A1' and other categories like 'double' or 'triple' plate appeared toward the end of the century with a host of confusing names, like Nevada silver, which is an American trade name. The proliferation of the latter gives us an indication of the huge import and export trade in silver and plate during the late Victorian period, making the subject even more complex and fascinating. At one time electroplate was scorned by all but the most far-sighted collectors, but more recently the true worth of such exquisite work by leading makers like Elkington Brothers and the *avant-garde* designs of Dr Christopher Dresser in the 1880s has been recognised. Indeed, Dr Dresser's pieces, looking in retrospect more like the 1930s, can make several thousands of pounds each.

In 1843 a refinement of the electroplating process called electrotyping was to kindle an interest in more naturalistic designs in silverware. In this method a mould is used – say for example a panel showing a complex battle scene with many figures in high relief – as one of the electrodes in the electroplating vat and is covered or 'lined' with either copper or silver to produce a precise replica again and again. This was yet another revolutionary technique which enabled the mass production of works of art in an age when craft turned to industry.

## Notable makers

Joseph Hancock began the development of Sheffield plate as an industry; and Henry Tudor of Tudor & Leader was the next important maker. Others included Roberts Cadman & Co of Sheffield and Matthew Boulton of Soho, Birmingham. Roberts Cadman & Co used the sign of a bell as their mark. Others makers' devices are crossed arrows (Fenton Creswick & Co), crossed keys in a shield (Henry Wilkinson & Co), a ship in full sail (Thomas Watson, Fenton & Bradbury), a phoenix (Kirkby, Waterhouse & Co), an elongated trumpet (A. Goodman & Co), and the most famous of all, two eight-pointed stars (Matthew Boulton).

(Above) A shaped circular salver of the Rococo period, the cast and applied border displaying several decorative features popular at this time, i.e. a deep Scotia moulded border and a finely moulded edge interspersed with formalised shells. (Below) The hallmarks on the salver are (from the left): the London date letter for 1740; the Crowned Leopard's Head, the London town mark; the maker's mark R.A. in script (for Robert Abercrombie); the Lion Passant, the sterling standard mark.

*A fine circular salver of the Classical period, decorated at the centre with bright-cut engraving for the cartouche around the coat of arms. The husk and double bead edge is embossed and applied. On later examples of Classical silver such decoration was achieved with bright-cut engraving only as embossing became less popular.*

*(Opposite top) The hallmarks on the underside of the salver above. From the left, they are: maker's mark for John Crouch and Thomas Hannam (inverted); the London date letter for 1781; the Lion Passant, which is the sterling mark; and the Crowned Leopard's Head, the London town mark. Also visible below the hallmarks is a scratched date, 1781.*

*(Opposite centre) A close-up of the outer edge of the same salver showing the simple but extremely effective method of embossing the husks within the two bead edges.*

*(Opposite bottom) The underside of the embossed edge showing the outer rim to be cast and applied. This gives additional strength to the border and usually signifies good quality.*

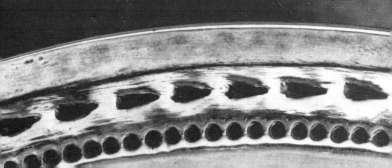

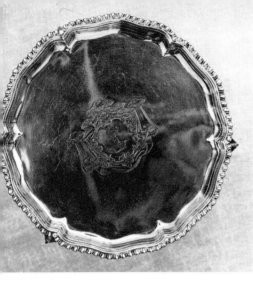

(Left) A shaped circular salver in the later Rococo style, the outer edge with gadroon decoration, engraved on the centre with a contemporary cartouche and what at first appears to be a suitable crest.

(Opposite top) The same salver, but with the centre area frosted. This dulls the surface and will assist in revealing any faults, joins or repairs. It is clear that a patch of different metal has been added to the centre, not easily discernible when the surface is highly polished. The effect of frosting can be achieved by breathing on the surface. It also enables easier recognition of the hallmarks. The reasons for the patch are discussed below and in the chapter on Fakes.

(Below) The hallmarks on the underside of the salver are, from the left: the London date letter for 1766; the Lion Passant; the Leopard's Head Crowned; and the maker's mark of Thomas Hannam and John Crouch. Also visible are the scratched figures 13..5. This is known as the scratch weight and was drawn on the silver at the time of manufacture. It can be useful when, after allowing for slight loss of weight through cleaning, it is possible to judge whether any serious omission or addition has occurred to the piece.

(Opposite bottom) The underside of the salver, the centre of which reveals a circular indentation where the silver has been beaten up to the top surface after erasing of previous crests. When the silver became too thin for further engraving it was again beaten down and the cavity filled with a hard white metal visible from the top when the surface has been frosted.

73 „ 5

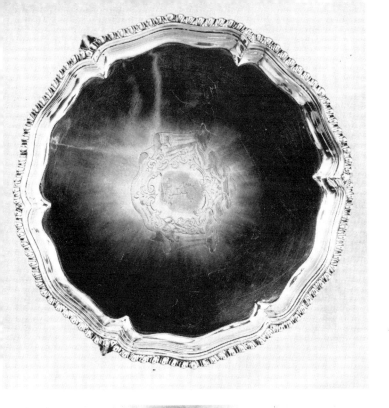

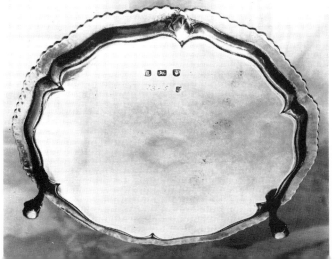

A pair of horn beakers with silver mounts, the borders decorated with bright-cut engraving in floral festoon designs.

A close-up of the marks on the silver mounts to the cups illustrated above. From the left they are: the duty mark, which is the Sovereign's Head in profile; the Lion Passant; and the London date letter of 1793. The maker's marks on both cup rims are slightly rubbed but comparison of the two suggests the initials A.F. The London town mark on this cup rim has been omitted.

*A pair of wine cups in the pure Classical form of the early nineteenth century. The engraving of arms without flamboyant cartouche is typical of this style in its severest application and the lobing to the lower body conforms with the decoration of the marble garden vases so popular during the late Georgian periods. London, 1825, by Emes and Barnard.*

*A four-bottle cruet stand in the Classical boat-shape design. This stand incorporates several features found in good-quality silver of its period: the cast and applied bead edge; the fluted pilaster supports to the upper frame; reeded loop handles; and cast panel feet. London, 1776, maker's mark A.F.*

*(Left) A vase-shape mustard pot in the slightly later Classical style incorporating pierced decoration and bright-cut engraving. Considerable decorative effect was achieved by using liners of deep blue glass for small container items such as mustard pots, salt cellars, sugar bowls and sweet-meat baskets during the late eighteenth and early nineteenth century. London, 1790, by Charles Haugham.*

*(Below) A fine example of a salt cellar in the pure Classical style of the late eighteenth century. The fluting to the lower half of the body is identical in design and quality to the candlesticks illustrated on page 43; it is by the same makers, Wakelin and Taylor, London, King's Head Intaglio duty mark and the date letter for 1784/5 (a small Roman type 'i').*

*(Bottom) An oval straight-sided salt cellar of the later Classical period showing similar decorative features to those of the mustard pot (top). Here the pierced work has a more geometric appearance over a simple but extremely effective use of bright-cut engraving. In contrast to the salt cellar above this example stands on four panel feet rather than the spread foot. Marked on the underside: London, 1789, maker's mark J.S. in script.*

(Above) A George III salver, one of a pair, showing the 'Chippendale' border and gadroon edge, 1767.

(Right) The marks on this salver are the Lion Passant sterling mark; the Leopard's Head London town mark; date letter 'M' 1767, and the maker's mark T. H. and I. C. Thomas Hannam and John Crouch.

(Above) A George III tea urn showing the Classic influence but retaining some Rococo style in the handles, 1774.

(Left) A George I tea kettle on heater base clearly showing the simple Rococo style, 1724.

*A typical George II cast candlestick, 10 inches high.*

*A George III candlestick in the pure Classic style, 12 inches high.*

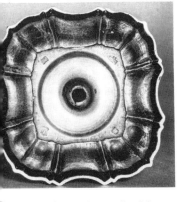

*The hallmarks on the candlestick above are placed in the corners underneath the base. London 1744. Wm. Gould.*

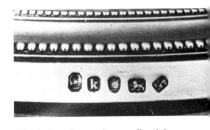

*The hallmarks on the candlestick above are placed on the outside bottom rim. Notice the Sovereign's Head mark intaglio. London 1785. J. Wakelin and Wm. Taylor.*

47

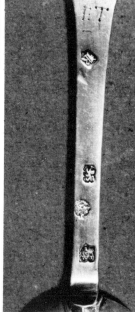

George II spoon. London 1759. (Letter 'D'.) Maker's mark N.K.

George II marrow scoop. London 1743. (Letter 'H'.) Unusual maker's mark with name in full F. King.

Charles II spoon. London 1667. (Letter 'K'.) Maker's mark W.I. with lion above.

Marks from a George III pen tray showing the Sovereign's Head duty mark. London 1800. (Letter 'E'.) Maker's name T.W., Thom Wallis.

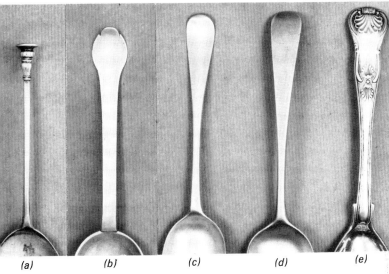

(a)       (b)       (c)       (d)       (e)

*From left to right: (a) a seal top spoon c. 1540, the design of which became 'slipped in the stem', then flattened as a Puritan spoon, then (b) widened out at the top c. 1670. Natural development produced the 'Old English' style handle (c) which sometimes curled down instead of up at the handle (d). Both were made throughout the eighteenth century; (e) a King's pattern spoon, generally made after 1800.*

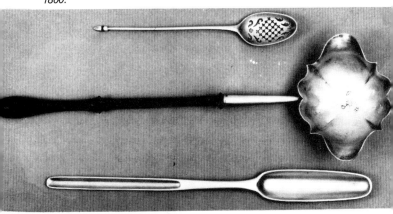

*Three articles of Georgian silver ideal for starting a collection. Top: a mote spoon, for skimming tea leaves from a cup of tea and for cleaning inside the pot with the pointed end. Centre: a double-lipped ladle, of which there are endless varieties and shapes. Bottom: a scoop for marrow bones.*

(Above) A double-sided ink-stand—there are two wells for pens. The bottle tops are made for a taper or small candle holder, ink-pot, and sand shaker. This shows the Empire influence on the feet but it retains the gadroon edge. London 1812.

(Right) A Victorian Rustic style mug, the naturalistic decoration forming the base, stem and handle. Birmingham 1857.

(Above) A George II lemon strainer, marked on both handles and inside the bowl. Dublin 1732. Matthew Alanson. In the bowl is the Crowned Harp for Dublin, the date letter 'M' of 1732, and Hibernia, a duty mark imposed on Irish silver in 1729 and equivalent to the Sovereign's Head on English silver which started in 1784.

(Left) An Art Nouveau style cup, showing the combination of decorative styles; inset semi-precious stones, Classic festoons, bands of acorns, rope twist edge, and Gothic lettering for the inscription. London 1922. Alwyn Carr.

*A collection of eighteenth- and early nineteenth-century items used in tea and coffee drinking. From left to right: a bullet-shape tea pot c. 1730; a Classic helmet-shape cream jug c. 1775; an oval sugar bowl c. 1790; a baluster-shape coffee pot c. 1765; a cut glass and silver-mounted tea caddy c. 1810. In the front is a mote spoon c. 1770 and a pair of sugar nips c. 1795. The tea table is Hepplewhite period c. 1770.*

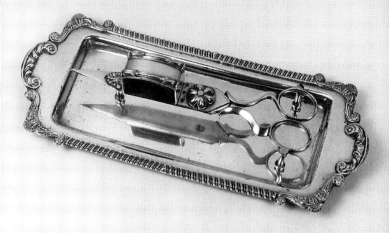

*A snuffer tray and scissor snuffers which exemplify the Sheffield plate industry in its more moderate domestic form, still receiving complex decoration and great attention to detail. The scissor snuffers are spring-loaded and the central box has a steel shutter which, when the scissors are opened, rises to allow the long and dangerous wick on a burning candle to be cut off and enclosed. The shutter falls like a guillotine to extinguish the smouldering end and prevent its falling out when the scissors are next opened. The base metal is nickel, with steel for the working parts, and the decorative mounts, i.e. the straps to the top of the box, the formalised palmette at the base of the spike and the rosette camouflaging the pinion, are lead-filled, stamped-out silver; the borders to the tray are spirally lobed, or gadrooned, on the long sides, culminating in two ends with Classic style C-scrolls, palmettes and gadroons, also silver and lead-filled and doubly secured with a roll-over edge, clearly apparent in the photograph (below) of the underside.*

*This shows the underside of the snuffer tray with the edges of the applied borders, rolled over in the traditional manner, clearly visible. Also visible are two of the four little feet, which are lead-filled. The darkened colour of the undersurface of such pieces is due to tinning. This was less expensive than double plating with silver but precluded exposure of the copper core. Tinning was used on the undersides of less expensive domestic items and the insides of cooking utensils.*

This is a fine example of a hot water urn dating from the mid 1820s. Here can be seen the various silver and lead-filled mounts applied separately and with age disclosing the disparate assembly. The feet and gadrooned borders to the base, the lion mask ring handles and the gadroon borders to the upper edges are of separate manufacture and applied to the already formed bowl, stem and base of the article. The lever to the tap is also manufactured in the same way with the finial fashioned as a formalised palmette, typical of the late Regency period; just visible behind this is a paler shade of metal indicating an oval Sterling silver plate 'let in' to the surface to receive an engraving of a monogram, cypher or coat of arms without disclosing the copper body of the piece.

# Tables of hallmarks

The following tables showing London, Birmingham and Sheffield assay marks are set out in full, with the exception of Sheffield where after 1780 the date letter applied on smaller articles had the crown incorporated either above the letter as shown (1802) or beside the letter, especially after 1829. The Crown appears upside down below the letter 'O' in 1815 and upside down above the letter from 1816 to 1820 – probably to clarify the difference between those years and 1793, 1797, 1798 and other year marks which may appear similar.

The tables showing the Chester, York, Newcastle and Exeter assay marks are condensed and intended as a guide to the changes in letter and shield shapes. However, it is possible to work out any given date letter using the same method of reading as for the preceding tables.

The Jubilee Mark, bearing the heads in profile of King George V and Queen Mary, commemorating the 25th anniversary of their accession to the throne, was used in 1933, 1934 and 1935.

The Coronation Mark, to commemorate the Coronation of Her Majesty Queen Elizabeth II and bearing the sovereign's head in profile, was used on silver plate for the years 1952 and 1953.

The Silver Jubilee Mark was used on items weighing fifteen grams or more that were hallmarked in 1977.

# LONDON

| | | | | | | | | | |
|---|---|---|---|---|---|---|---|---|---|
| 1658 | | | | 1682 | | | | 1705 | |
| 1659 | ,, | ,, | | 1683 | ,, | ,, | | 1706 | ,, | ,, |
| 1660 | ,, | ,, | | 1684 | ,, | ,, | | 1707 | ,, | ,, |
| 1661 | ,, | ,, | | 1685 | ,, | ,, | | 1708 | ,, | ,, |
| 1662 | ,, | ,, | | 1686 | ,, | ,, | | 1709 | ,, | ,, |
| 1663 | ,, | ,, | | 1687 | ,, | ,, | | 1710 | ,, | ,, |
| 1664 | ,, | ,, | | 1688 | ,, | ,, | | 1711 | ,, | ,, |
| 1665 | ,, | ,, | | 1689 | ,, | ,, | | 1712 | ,, | ,, |
| 1666 | ,, | ,, | | 1690 | ,, | ,, | | 1713 | ,, | ,, |
| 1667 | ,, | ,, | | 1691 | ,, | ,, | | 1714 | ,, | ,, |
| 1668 | ,, | ,, | | 1692 | ,, | ,, | | 1715 | ,, | ,, |
| 1669 | ,, | ,, | | 1693 | ,, | ,, | | | | |
| 1670 | ,, | ,, | | 1694 | ,, | ,, | | 1716 | | |
| 1671 | ,, | ,, | | 1695 | ,, | ,, | | 1717 | ,, | ,, |
| 1672 | ,, | ,, | | 1696 | ,, | ,, | | 1718 | ,, | ,, |
| 1673 | ,, | ,, | | | | | | 1719 | ,, | ,, |
| 1674 | ,, | ,, | | 1697 | | | | 1720 | | |
| 1675 | ,, | ,, | | | ,, | ,, | | 1721 | | |
| 1676 | ,, | ,, | | 1698 | ,, | ,, | | 1722 | ,, | ,, |
| 1677 | ,, | ,, | | 1699 | ,, | ,, | | 1723 | ,, | ,, |
| | | | | 1700 | ,, | ,, | | 1724 | | ,, |
| 1678 | | | | 1701 | ,, | ,, | | 1725 | ,, | ,, |
| 1679 | | | | 1702 | ,, | ,, | | 1726 | ,, | ,, |
| 1680 | ,, | ,, | | 1703 | ,, | ,, | | 1727 | ,, | ,, |
| 1681 | ,, | ,, | | 1704 | ,, | ,, | | 1728 | ,, | ,, |

# LONDON

| Year | | | Mark | Year | | | Mark | Year | | | Mark |
|------|--|--|------|------|--|--|------|------|--|--|------|
| 1729 | | | O | 1753 | | | I | 1776 | | | a |
| 1730 | ,, | ,, | P | 1754 | ,, | ,, | t | 1777 | ,, | ,, | b |
| 1731 | ,, | ,, | Q | 1755 | ,, | ,, | u | 1778 | ,, | ,, | c |
| 1732 | ,, | ,, | R | | | | | 1779 | ,, | ,, | d |
| 1733 | ,, | ,, | S | 1756 | | | A | 1780 | ,, | ,, | e |
| 1734 | ,, | ,, | T | 1757 | ,, | ,, | B | 1781 | ,, | ,, | f |
| 1735 | ,, | ,, | V | 1758 | ,, | ,, | C | 1782 | ,, | ,, | g |
| | | | | 1759 | ,, | ,, | D | 1783 | ,, | ,, | h |
| 1736 | | | a | 1760 | ,, | ,, | E | 1784 | ,, | ,, | i |
| 1737 | ,, | ,, | b | 1761 | ,, | ,, | F | 1785 | ,, | ,, | k |
| 1738 | ,, | ,, | C | 1762 | ,, | ,, | G | 1786 | ,, | ,, | l |
| 1739 | ,, | ,, | d | 1763 | ,, | ,, | H | 1787 | ,, | ,, | m |
| 1740 | ,, | ,, | e | 1764 | ,, | ,, | I | 1788 | ,, | ,, | n |
| 1741 | ,, | ,, | f | 1765 | ,, | ,, | K | 1789 | ,, | ,, | o |
| 1742 | ,, | ,, | g | 1766 | ,, | ,, | L | 1790 | ,, | ,, | p |
| 1743 | ,, | ,, | h | 1767 | ,, | ,, | M | 1791 | ,, | ,, | q |
| 1744 | ,, | ,, | i | 1768 | ,, | ,, | N | 1792 | ,, | ,, | r |
| 1745 | ,, | ,, | k | 1769 | ,, | ,, | O | 1793 | ,, | ,, | s |
| 1746 | ,, | ,, | l | 1770 | ,, | ,, | P | 1794 | ,, | ,, | t |
| 1747 | ,, | ,, | m | 1771 | ,, | ,, | Q | 1795 | ,, | ,, | u |
| 1748 | ,, | ,, | n | 1772 | ,, | ,, | R | | | | |
| 1749 | ,, | ,, | O | 1773 | ,, | ,, | S | 1796 | | | A |
| 1750 | ,, | ,, | P | 1774 | ,, | ,, | T | 1797 | ,, | ,, | B |
| 1751 | ,, | ,, | q | 1775 | ,, | ,, | U | 1798 | ,, | ,, | C |
| 1752 | ,, | ,, | r | | | | | | | | |

# LONDON

| 1799 | 👑 | 🦁 | 👤 | **D** | 1822 | 👑 | 🦁 | 👤 | **g** | 1845 | 👑 | 🦁 | 👤 | **K** |
|------|---|---|---|---|------|---|---|---|---|------|---|---|---|---|
| 1800 | ,, | ,, | ,, | **E** | 1823 | ,, | ,, | ,, | **h** | 1846 | ,, | ,, | ,, | **L** |
| 1801 | ,, | ,, | ,, | **F** | 1824 | ,, | ,, | ,, | **i** | 1847 | ,, | ,, | ,, | **M** |
| 1802 | ,, | ,, | ,, | **G** | 1825 | ,, | ,, | ,, | **k** | 1848 | ,, | ,, | ,, | **N** |
| 1803 | ,, | ,, | ,, | **H** | 1826 | ,, | ,, | ,, | **l** | 1849 | ,, | ,, | ,, | **O** |
| 1804 | ,, | ,, | ,, | **I** | 1827 | ,, | ,, | ,, | **m** | 1850 | ,, | ,, | ,, | **P** |
| 1805 | ,, | ,, | ,, | **K** | 1828 | ,, | ,, | ,, | **n** | 1851 | ,, | ,, | ,, | **Q** |
| 1806 | ,, | ,, | ,, | **L** | 1829 | ,, | ,, | ,, | **o** | 1852 | ,, | ,, | ,, | **R** |
| 1807 | ,, | ,, | ,, | **M** | 1830 | ,, | ,, | ,, | **p** | 1853 | ,, | ,, | ,, | **S** |
| 1808 | ,, | ,, | ,, | **N** | 1831 | ,, | ,, | ,, | **q** | 1854 | ,, | ,, | ,, | **T** |
| 1809 | ,, | ,, | ,, | **O** | 1832 | ,, | ,, | ,, | **r** | 1855 | ,, | ,, | ,, | **U** |
| 1810 | ,, | ,, | ,, | **P** | 1833 | ,, | ,, | ,, | **s** | | | | | |
| 1811 | ,, | ,, | ,, | **Q** | 1834 | ,, | ,, | 👤 | **t** | | | | | |
| 1812 | ,, | ,, | ,, | **R** | 1835 | ,, | ,, | ,, | **u** | 1856 | 🦁 | 🦁 | 👤 | **a** |
| 1813 | ,, | ,, | ,, | **S** | | | | | | 1857 | ,, | ,, | ,, | **b** |
| 1814 | ,, | ,, | ,, | **T** | | | | | | 1858 | ,, | ,, | ,, | **c** |
| 1815 | ,, | ,, | ,, | **U** | 1836 | 👑 | 🦁 | 👤 | **A** | 1859 | ,, | ,, | ,, | **d** |
| | | | | | 1837 | ,, | ,, | ,, | **B** | 1860 | ,, | ,, | ,, | **e** |
| | | | | | 1838 | ,, | ,, | 👤 | **C** | 1861 | ,, | ,, | ,, | **f** |
| 1816 | 👑 | 🦁 | 👤 | **a** | 1839 | ,, | ,, | ,, | **D** | 1862 | ,, | ,, | ,, | **g** |
| 1817 | ,, | ,, | ,, | **b** | 1840 | ,, | ,, | ,, | **E** | 1863 | ,, | ,, | ,, | **h** |
| 1818 | ,, | ,, | ,, | **C** | 1841 | ,, | ,, | ,, | **F** | 1864 | ,, | ,, | ,, | **i** |
| 1819 | ,, | ,, | ,, | **d** | 1842 | ,, | ,, | ,, | **G** | 1865 | ,, | ,, | ,, | **k** |
| 1820 | ,, | ,, | ,, | **e** | 1843 | ,, | ,, | ,, | **H** | 1866 | ,, | ,, | ,, | **l** |
| 1821 | 🦁 | 🦁 | 👤 | **f** | 1844 | ,, | ,, | ,, | **J** | 1867 | ,, | ,, | ,, | **m** |

## LONDON

| Year | | | | | Year | | | | | Year | | | |
|---|---|---|---|---|---|---|---|---|---|---|---|---|---|
| 1868 | 🦁 | 🦁 | 👑 | n | 1891 | 👑 | 🦁 | | Q | 1914 | 🦁 | 🦁 | t |
| 1869 | ,, | ,, | ,, | o | 1892 | ,, | ,, | | R | 1915 | ,, | ,, | u |
| 1870 | ,, | ,, | ,, | p | 1893 | ,, | ,, | | S | | | | |
| 1871 | ,, | ,, | ,, | q | 1894 | ,, | ,, | | T | | | | |
| 1872 | ,, | ,, | ,, | r | 1895 | ,, | ,, | | U | 1916 | 👑 | 🦁 | a |
| 1873 | ,, | ,, | ,, | s | | | | | | 1917 | ,, | ,, | b |
| 1874 | ,, | ,, | ,, | t | 1896 | 🦁 | 🦁 | a | | 1918 | ,, | ,, | c |
| 1875 | ,, | ,, | ,, | u | 1897 | ,, | ,, | b | | 1919 | ,, | ,, | d |
| | | | | | 1898 | ,, | ,, | c | | 1920 | ,, | ,, | e |
| 1876 | 👑 | 🦁 | 👑 | A | 1899 | ,, | ,, | d | | 1921 | ,, | ,, | f |
| 1877 | ,, | ,, | ,, | B | 1900 | ,, | ,, | e | | 1922 | ,, | ,, | g |
| 1878 | ,, | ,, | ,, | C | 1901 | ,, | ,, | f | | 1923 | ,, | ,, | h |
| 1879 | ,, | ,, | ,, | D | 1902 | ,, | ,, | g | | 1924 | ,, | ,, | i |
| 1880 | ,, | ,, | ,, | E | 1903 | ,, | ,, | h | | 1925 | ,, | ,, | k |
| 1881 | ,, | ,, | ,, | F | 1904 | ,, | ,, | i | | 1926 | ,, | ,, | l |
| 1882 | ,, | ,, | ,, | G | 1905 | ,, | ,, | k | | 1927 | ,, | ,, | m |
| 1883 | ,, | ,, | ,, | H | 1906 | ,, | ,, | l | | 1928 | ,, | ,, | n |
| 1884 | ,, | ,, | ,, | I | 1907 | ,, | ,, | m | | 1929 | ,, | ,, | o |
| 1885 | ,, | ,, | ,, | K | 1908 | ,, | ,, | n | | 1930 | ,, | ,, | p |
| 1886 | ,, | ,, | ,, | L | 1909 | ,, | ,, | o | | 1931 | ,, | ,, | q |
| 1887 | ,, | ,, | ,, | M | 1910 | ,, | ,, | p | | 1932 | ,, | ,, | r |
| 1888 | ,, | ,, | ,, | N | 1911 | ,, | ,, | q | | 1933 | ,, | ,, | 👑 s |
| 1889 | ,, | ,, | ,, | O | 1912 | ,, | ,, | r | | 1934 | ,, | ,, | t |
| 1890 | ,, | ,, | ,, | P | 1913 | ,, | ,, | s | | 1935 | ,, | ,, | u |

# LONDON

| Year | | | Mark | Year | | | Mark | Year | | | Mark |
|------|---|---|------|------|---|---|------|------|---|---|------|
| 1936 | | | A | 1960 | | | e | 1984 | | | K |
| 1937 | ,, | ,, | B | 1961 | ,, | ,, | f | 1985 | ,, | ,, | L |
| 1938 | ,, | ,, | C | 1962 | ,, | ,, | g | 1986 | ,, | ,, | M |
| 1939 | ,, | ,, | D | 1963 | ,, | ,, | h | 1987 | ,, | ,, | N |
| 1940 | ,, | ,, | E | 1964 | ,, | ,, | i | 1988 | ,, | ,, | O |
| 1941 | ,, | ,, | F | 1965 | ,, | ,, | k | 1989 | ,, | ,, | P |
| 1942 | ,, | ,, | G | 1966 | ,, | ,, | l | 1990 | ,, | ,, | Q |
| 1943 | ,, | ,, | H | 1967 | ,, | ,, | m | 1991 | ,, | ,, | R |
| 1944 | ,, | ,, | I | 1968 | ,, | ,, | n | 1992 | ,, | ,, | S |
| 1945 | ,, | ,, | K | 1969 | ,, | ,, | o | 1993 | ,, | ,, | T |
| 1946 | ,, | ,, | L | 1970 | ,, | ,, | p | 1994 | ,, | ,, | U |
| 1947 | ,, | ,, | M | 1971 | ,, | ,, | q | 1995 | ,, | ,, | V |
| 1948 | ,, | ,, | N | 1972 | ,, | ,, | r | 1996 | ,, | ,, | W |
| 1949 | ,, | ,, | O | 1973 | ,, | ,, | s | 1997 | ,, | ,, | X |
| 1950 | ,, | ,, | P | 1974 | ,, | ,, | t | 1998 | ,, | ,, | Y |
| 1951 | ,, | ,, | Q | 1975 | | | A | 1999 | ,, | ,, | Z |
| 1952 | ,, | ,, | R | 1976 | ,, | ,, | B | 2000 | ,, | ,, | a |
| 1953 | ,, | ,, | S | 1977 | ,, | ,, | C | 2001 | ,, | ,, | b |
| 1954 | ,, | ,, | T | 1978 | ,, | ,, | D | 2002 | ,, | ,, | c |
| 1955 | ,, | ,, | U | 1979 | ,, | ,, | E | 2003 | ,, | ,, | d |
| 1956 | ,, | ,, | a | 1980 | ,, | ,, | F | 2004 | ,, | ,, | e |
| 1957 | ,, | ,, | b | 1981 | ,, | ,, | G | 2005 | ,, | ,, | f |
| 1958 | ,, | ,, | c | 1982 | ,, | ,, | H | 2006 | ,, | ,, | g |
| 1959 | ,, | ,, | d | 1983 | ,, | ,, | J | and continuing to 'Z' (2024) | | | |

## BIRMINGHAM

| | | | | | | | | | | | | |
|---|---|---|---|---|---|---|---|---|---|---|---|---|
| 1773 | 🦁 | ⚓ | | **A** | 1796 | 🦁 | ⚓ | 👤 | **Y** | 1818 | 🦁 ⚓ 👤 | **u** |
| 1774 | ,, | ,, | | **B** | 1797 | ,, | ,, | ,, | **Z** | 1819 | ,, ,, ,, | **v** |
| 1775 | ,, | ,, | | **C** | | | | | | 1820 | ,, ,, ,, | **W** |
| 1776 | ,, | ,, | | **D** | | | | | | 1821 | ,, ,, ,, | **X** |
| 1777 | ,, | ,, | | **E** | 1798 | 🦁 | ⚓ | 👤 | **a** | 1822 | ,, ,, ,, | **y** |
| 1778 | ,, | ,, | | **F** | 1799 | ,, | ,, | ,, | **b** | 1823 | ,, ,, ,, | **Z** |
| 1779 | ,, | ,, | | **G** | 1800 | ,, | ,, | ,, | **C** | | | |
| 1780 | ,, | ,, | | **H** | 1801 | ,, | ,, | ,, | **d** | | | |
| 1781 | ,, | ,, | | **I** | 1802 | ,, | ,, | ,, | **e** | 1824 | 🦁 ⚓ 👤 | **A** |
| 1782 | ,, | ,, | | **K** | 1803 | ,, | ,, | ,, | **f** | 1825 | ,, ,, ,, | **B** |
| 1783 | ,, | ,, | | **L** | 1804 | ,, | ,, | ,, | **g** | 1826 | ,, ,, ,, | **C** |
| 1784 | ,, | ,, | 👤 | **M** | 1805 | ,, | ,, | ,, | **h** | 1827 | ,, ,, ,, | **D** |
| 1785 | ,, | ,, | ,, | **N** | 1806 | ,, | ,, | ,, | **i** | 1828 | ,, ,, ,, | **E** |
| 1786 | ,, | ,, | 👤 | **O** | 1807 | ,, | ,, | ,, | **j** | 1829 | ,, ,, ,, | **F** |
| 1787 | ,, | ,, | ,, | **P** | 1808 | ,, | ,, | ,, | **k** | 1830 | ,, ,, ,, | **G** |
| 1788 | ,, | ,, | ,, | **Q** | 1809 | ,, | ,, | ,, | **l** | 1831 | ,, ,, ,, | **H** |
| 1789 | ,, | ,, | ,, | **R** | 1810 | ,, | ,, | ,, | **m** | 1832 | ,, ,, ,, | **J** |
| 1790 | ,, | ,, | ,, | **S** | 1811 | ,, | ,, | ,, | **n** | 1833 | ,, ,, ,, | **K** |
| 1791 | ,, | ,, | ,, | **T** | 1812 | ,, | ,, | ,, | **o** | 1834 | ,, ,, ,, | **L** |
| 1792 | ,, | ,, | ,, | **U** | 1813 | ,, | ,, | ,, | **p** | 1835 | ,, ,, ,, | **M** |
| 1793 | ,, | ,, | ,, | **V** | 1814 | ,, | ,, | ,, | **q** | 1836 | ,, ,, ,, | **N** |
| 1794 | ,, | ,, | ,, | **W** | 1815 | ,, | ,, | ,, | **r** | 1837 | ,, ,, ,, | **O** |
| 1795 | ,, | ,, | ,, | **X** | 1816 | ,, | ,, | ,, | **s** | 1838 | ,, ,, 👤 | **P** |
| | | | | | 1817 | ,, | ,, | ,, | **t** | 1839 | ,, ,, ,, | **Q** |

# BIRMINGHAM

| Year | Date Letter | Year | Date Letter | Year | Date Letter |
|---|---|---|---|---|---|
| 1840 | 𝕽 | 1862 | N | 1884 | k |
| 1841 | S | 1863 | O | 1885 | l |
| 1842 | T | 1864 | P | 1886 | m |
| 1843 | U | 1865 | Q | 1887 | n |
| 1844 | V | 1866 | R | 1888 | o |
| 1845 | W | 1867 | S | 1889 | p |
| 1846 | X | 1868 | T | 1890 | q |
| 1847 | Y | 1869 | U | 1891 | r |
| 1848 | Z | 1870 | V | 1892 | s |
| — | — | 1871 | W | 1893 | t |
| 1849 | A | 1872 | X | 1894 | u |
| 1850 | B | 1873 | Y | 1895 | v |
| 1851 | C | 1874 | Z | 1896 | w |
| 1852 | D | — | — | 1897 | x |
| 1853 | E | 1875 | a | 1898 | y |
| 1854 | F | 1876 | b | 1899 | z |
| 1855 | G | 1877 | c | — | — |
| 1856 | H | 1878 | d | 1900 | a |
| 1857 | I | 1879 | e | 1901 | b |
| 1858 | J | 1880 | f | 1902 | c |
| 1859 | K | 1881 | g | 1903 | d |
| 1860 | L | 1882 | h | 1904 | e |
| 1861 | M | 1883 | i | 1905 | f |

# BIRMINGHAM

| Year | | | Letter | Year | | | Letter | Year | | | Letter |
|---|---|---|---|---|---|---|---|---|---|---|---|
| 1906 | | | g | 1931 | | | G | 1957 | | | H |
| 1907 | ,, | ,, | h | 1932 | ,, | ,, | H | 1958 | ,, | ,, | I |
| 1908 | ,, | ,, | i | 1933 | | | J | 1959 | ,, | ,, | K |
| 1909 | ,, | ,, | k | 1934 | ,, | ,, | K | 1960 | ,, | ,, | L |
| 1910 | ,, | ,, | l | 1935 | ,, | ,, | L | 1961 | ,, | ,, | M |
| 1911 | ,, | ,, | m | 1936 | ,, | ,, | M | 1962 | ,, | ,, | N |
| 1912 | ,, | ,, | n | 1937 | ,, | ,, | N | 1963 | ,, | ,, | O |
| 1913 | ,, | ,, | o | 1938 | ,, | ,, | O | 1964 | ,, | ,, | P |
| 1914 | ,, | ,, | p | 1939 | ,, | ,, | P | 1965 | ,, | ,, | Q |
| 1915 | ,, | ,, | q | 1940 | ,, | ,, | Q | 1966 | ,, | ,, | R |
| 1916 | ,, | ,, | r | 1941 | ,, | ,, | R | 1967 | ,, | ,, | S |
| 1917 | ,, | ,, | s | 1942 | ,, | ,, | S | 1968 | ,, | ,, | T |
| 1918 | ,, | ,, | t | 1943 | ,, | ,, | T | 1969 | ,, | ,, | U |
| 1919 | ,, | ,, | u | 1944 | ,, | ,, | U | 1970 | ,, | ,, | V |
| 1920 | ,, | ,, | v | 1945 | ,, | ,, | V | 1971 | ,, | ,, | W |
| 1921 | ,, | ,, | w | 1946 | ,, | ,, | W | 1972 | ,, | ,, | X |
| 1922 | ,, | ,, | x | 1947 | ,, | ,, | X | 1973 | ,, | ,, | Y |
| 1923 | ,, | ,, | y | 1948 | ,, | ,, | Y | 1974 | ,, | ,, | Z |
| 1924 | ,, | ,, | z | 1949 | ,, | ,, | Z | 1975 | | | A |
| 1925 | ,, | ,, | A | 1950 | | | A | 1976 | ,, | ,, | B |
| 1926 | ,, | ,, | B | 1951 | ,, | ,, | B | 1977 | ,, | ,, | C |
| 1927 | ,, | ,, | C | 1952 | ,, | ,, | C | 1978 | ,, | ,, | D |
| 1928 | ,, | ,, | D | 1953 | ,, | ,, | D | 1979 | ,, | ,, | E |
| 1929 | ,, | ,, | E | 1954 | ,, | ,, | E | 1980 | ,, | ,, | F |
| 1930 | ,, | ,, | F | 1955 | ,, | ,, | F | 1981 | ,, | ,, | G |
| | | | | 1956 | ,, | ,, | G | 1982 | ,, | ,, | H |

Subsequent date
letters as for London.

# CHESTER

| Year | Marks | Letter | Year | Marks | Letter | Year | Marks | Letter |
|---|---|---|---|---|---|---|---|---|
| 1701 | | A | 1777 | | b | 1901 | | A |
| 1702 | ,, ,, ,, | B | 1778 | ,, ,, ,, | C | 1902 | ,, ,, | B |
| 1703 | ,, ,, | C | 1779 | | d | similar shields to 1925 ,, ,, | | Z |
| 1704 | ,, ,, | D | 1780 | | e | 1926 | ,, ,, | J |
| 1705 | ,, ,, | E | similar shields to 1784 | | i | similar shields to 1933 | ,, ,, | H |
| similar shields to 1718 | ,, ,, | S | 1785 | ,, ,, ,, | k | 1934 | ,, ,, ,, | I |
| 1719 | | T | 1786 | ,, ,, | l | 1935 | ,, ,, ,, | K |
| 1720 | ,, ,, ,, | U | 1787 | ,, ,, ,, ,, | m | 1936 | ,, ,, ,, | L |
| similar shields to 1725 | ,, ,, ,, | Z | similar shields to 1796 | ,, ,, ,, ,, | V | 1937 | ,, ,, ,, | M |
| 1726 | | A | 1797 | ,, | A | 1938 | ,, ,, ,, | N |
| 1727 | ,, ,, ,, | B | 1798 | ,, ,, ,, | B | 1939 | ,, ,, ,, | O |
| similar shields to 1750 | ,, ,, | Z | 1799 | ,, ,, ,, | C | 1940 | ,, ,, ,, | P |
| 1751 | | a | similar shields to 1817 | ,, ,, ,, | V | 1941 | ,, ,, ,, | Q |
| 1752 | ,, ,, ,, | b | 1818 | | A | 1942 | ,, ,, ,, | R |
| similar shields to 1766 | ,, ,, ,, | Q | 1819 | ,, ,, ,, | B | 1943 | ,, ,, ,, | S |
| 1767 | ,, ,, ,, | R | similar shields to 1823 | | E | 1944 | ,, ,, ,, | T |
| 1768 | ,, ,, ,, | S | 1824 | ,, ,, ,, | F | 1945 | ,, ,, ,, | U |
| 1769 1770 | ,, ,, ,, ,, ,, ,, | T | similar shields to 1838 | ,, ,, ,, | U | 1946 | ,, ,, ,, | V |
| 1771 | ,, ,, ,, | U | 1839 | | A | 1947 | ,, ,, ,, | W |
| 1772 | ,, ,, ,, | V | 1840 | ,, ,, ,, | B | 1948 | ,, ,, ,, | X |
| 1773 | ,, ,, ,, | W | similar shields to 1863 | ,, ,, ,, | Z | 1949 | ,, ,, ,, | Y |
| 1774 | ,, ,, ,, | X | 1864 | ,, ,, ,, | a | 1950 | ,, ,, ,, | Z |
| 1775 | ,, ,, ,, | Y | similar shields to 1883 | ,, ,, ,, | u | 1951 | ,, ,, ,, | A |
| 1776 | ,, ,, ,, | a | 1884 | | A | 1952 | ,, ,, | B |
| | | | similar shields to 1900 | ,, ,, ,, | R | similar shields to 1962 | ,, ,, ,, | C M |

## EXETER

| Year | | | | Letter | | Year | | | | Letter | | Year | | | | Letter |
|---|---|---|---|---|---|---|---|---|---|---|---|---|---|---|---|---|
| 1701 | | | | A | | 1791 | | | | f | | 1830 | | | | O |
| 1702 | " | " | " | B | | 1792 | " | " | " | t | | 1831 | | " | " | p |
| *similar shields to* | | | | | | 1793 | " | " | " | u | | 1832 | | " | " | q |
| 1720 | " | " | " | V | | 1794 | " | " | " | w | | 1833 | | | | r |
| 1721 | | | | W | | 1795 | " | " | " | x | | *similar shields to* | | | | |
| *similar shields to* | | | | | | 1796 | " | " | " | y | | 1836 | " | " | " | u |
| 1724 | " | " | " | Z | | 1797 | | | | A | | 1837 | | | | A |
| 1725 | " | " | " | a | | 1798 | " | " | " | B | | 1838 | " | " | | B |
| *similar shields to* | | | | | | 1799 | " | " | | C | | 1839 | " | " | " | C |
| 1748 | " | " | " | z | | 1800 | " | " | " | D | | 1840 | " | " | " | D |
| 1749 | " | " | " | A | | *similar shields to* | | | | | | 1841 | | | | E |
| *similar shields to* | | | | | | 1805 | | | | I | | 1842 | " | " | " | f |
| 1759 | " | " | " | L | | *similar shields to* | | | | | | 1843 | | | | G |
| 1760 | " | " | " | M | | 1816 | " | " | " | U | | *similar shields to* | | | | |
| *similar shields to* | | | | | | 1817 | | | | a | | 1856 | " | " | " | H |
| 1768 | " | " | " | U | | 1818 | " | | " | b | | 1857 | | | | A |
| 1769 | " | " | " | W | | 1819 | " | " | " | c | | 1858 | " | " | " | B |
| 1770 | " | " | " | X | | 1820 | " | " | " | d | | 1859 | " | " | " | C |
| 1771 | " | " | " | Y | | 1821 | " | " | " | e | | 1860 | " | " | " | D |
| 1772 | " | " | " | Z | | 1822 | " | " | " | f | | *similar shields to* | | | | |
| 1773 | | | | A | | 1823 | " | " | " | g | | 1876 | " | " | " | U |
| *similar shields to* | | | | | | 1824 | " | " | " | h | | 1877 | | | | A |
| 1778 | " | " | " | F | | 1825 | " | " | " | i | | 1878 | " | " | " | B |
| 1779 | " | " | " | G | | 1826 | " | " | " | k | | 1879 | " | " | " | C |
| *similar shields to* | | | | | | 1827 | " | " | " | l | | 1880 | " | " | " | D |
| 1784 | " | " | " | L | | 1828 | " | " | " | m | | 1881 | " | " | " | E |
| 1785 | " | " | " | M | | 1829 | " | " | " | n | | 1882 | " | " | " | F |
| 1786 | " | " | | N | | | | | | | | | | | | |
| 1787 | " | " | " | O | | | | | | | | | | | | |
| 1788 | " | " | " | P | | | | | | | | | | | | |
| 1789 | " | " | " | q | | | | | | | | | | | | |
| 1790 | " | " | " | r | | | | | | | | | | | | |

# NEWCASTLE

| Year | Marks | | | | Year | Marks | | | | Year | Marks | | | |
|---|---|---|---|---|---|---|---|---|---|---|---|---|---|---|
| 1702 | | | | A | 1740 | | | | A | 1800 | | | | | K |
| 1703 | " | " | " | B | 1741 | " | " | " | B | 1801 | " | " | " | " | L |
| 1704 | " | " | " | C | 1742 | " | " | " | C | 1802 | " | " | " | " | M |
| 1705 | " | " | " | D | 1757 | similar shields to " " " | | | S | 1803 | " | " | " | | N |
| 1706 | " | " | " | E | 1758 | (assumed) | | | T | 1804 | " | " | " | " | O |
| 1707 | " | " | " | F | 1759 | " | " | " | A | 1805 | " | " | " | " | P |
| 1708 | " | " | " | G | 1760–8 | " | " | " | B | 1806 | " | " | " | " | Q |
| 1709 – 1711 No records available. | | | | | 1769 | " | " | " | C | 1807 | " | " | " | " | R |
| 1712 " " " D | | | | | 1770 | " | " | " | D | 1808 | " | " | " | " | S |
| 1713 No records. | | | | | 1771 | " | " | " | E | 1809 | " | " | " | " | T |
| 1714 | | | | D | 1772 | " | " | " | F | 1810 | " | " | " | " | U |
| 1715 – 1716 No records available. | | | | | 1773 | | | | G | 1811 | " | " | " | " | W |
| 1717 | " | " | " | P | 1779 | similar shields to " " " | | | N | 1812 | " | " | " | " | X |
| 1718 | " | " | " | Q | 1780 | " | " | " | O | 1813 | " | " | " | " | Y |
| 1719 | " | " | " | D | 1781 | " | " | " | P | 1814 | " | " | " | " | Z |
| 1720 | " | " | " | E | 1782 | " | " | " | Q | 1815 | " | " | " | " | A |
| 1721 | | | | a | 1783 | " | " | " | R | 1838 | similar shields to " " " " | | | | A |
| 1722 " " " B | | | | | 1784 | " | " | | S | 1839 | " | " | " | " | A |
| similar shields to | | | | | 1785 | " | " | " | T | 1840 | " | " | " | " | B |
| 1727 " " " C | | | | | 1786 | " | " | | U | 1841 | " | " | " | | C |
| 1728 | | | | h | 1787 | " | " | " | W | similar shields to | | | | | |
| 1729 " " " J | | | | | similar shields to | | | | | 1846 | | | | | C |
| similar shields to | | | | | 1790 | " | " | " | Z | 1847 | " | " | " | " | H |
| 1733 " " " N | | | | | 1791 | | | | A | similar shields to | | | | | |
| 1734 " " " O | | | | | 1792 " " " B | | | | | 1863 | " | " | " | " | Z |
| similar shields to | | | | | similar shields to | | | | | 1864 | " | " | " | " | a |
| 1737 " " " R | | | | | 1799 " " " " I | | | | | similar shields to | | | | | |
| 1738 " " S | | | | | | | | | | 1883 | " | " | " | " | u |
| 1739 " " " T | | | | | | | | | | | | | | | |

66

## SHEFFIELD

| Year | | | | | Year | | | | | Year | | | | |
|---|---|---|---|---|---|---|---|---|---|---|---|---|---|---|
| 1773 | 🦁 | 👑 | | 𝕰 | 1797 | 🦁 | 👑 | 😊 | X | 1820 | 🦁 | 👑 | 😊 | Q |
| 1774 | ,, | 👑 | | 𝕱 | | *On smaller objects a crown appears above the date letter. e.g. 1802* | | | | 1821 | ,, | ,, | ,, | Y |
| 1775 | ,, | ,, | | 𝕹 | 1798 | 🦁 | 👑 | 😊 | V | 1822 | ,, | ,, | ,, | Z |
| 1776 | ,, | ,, | | 𝕽 | 1799 | ,, | ,, | ,, | E | 1823 | ,, | ,, | ,, | U |
| 1777 | ,, | ,, | | 𝖍 | 1800 | ,, | ,, | ,, | N | 1824 | ,, | 👑 | ,, | a |
| 1778 | ,, | ,, | | 𝕾 | 1801 | ,, | ,, | ,, | H | 1825 | ,, | ,, | ,, | b |
| 1779 | ,, | ,, | | 𝕬 | 1802 | ,, | ,, | ,, | M̂ | 1826 | ,, | ,, | ,, | c |
| 1780 | ,, | ,, | | 𝕿 | 1803 | ,, | ,, | ,, | F | 1827 | ,, | ,, | ,, | d |
| 1781 | ,, | ,, | | 𝕯 | 1804 | ,, | ,, | ,, | G | 1828 | ,, | ,, | ,, | e |
| 1782 | ,, | ,, | | 𝕲 | 1805 | ,, | ,, | ,, | B | 1829 | ,, | ,, | ,, | f |
| 1783 | ,, | ,, | | 𝕭 | 1806 | ,, | ,, | ,, | A | 1830 | ,, | ,, | ,, | g |
| 1784 | ,, | ,, | 👤 | 𝕴 | 1807 | ,, | ,, | ,, | S | 1831 | ,, | ,, | ,, | h |
| 1785 | ,, | ,, | ,, | 𝖁 | 1808 | ,, | ,, | ,, | P | 1832 | ,, | ,, | ,, | k |
| 1786 | ,, | ,, | 😊 | 𝖐 | 1809 | ,, | ,, | ,, | K | 1833 | ,, | ,, | ,, | l |
| 1787 | ,, | ,, | ,, | 𝕮 | 1810 | ,, | ,, | ,, | L | 1834 | ,, | ,, | ,, | m |
| 1788 | ,, | ,, | ,, | 𝖜 | 1811 | ,, | ,, | ,, | C | 1835 | ,, | ,, | ,, | p |
| 1789 | ,, | ,, | ,, | 𝖒 | 1812 | ,, | ,, | ,, | D | 1836 | ,, | ,, | ,, | q |
| 1790 | ,, | ,, | ,, | 𝕷 | 1813 | ,, | ,, | ,, | R | 1837 | ,, | ,, | 😊 | r |
| 1791 | ,, | ,, | ,, | 𝕻 | 1814 | ,, | ,, | 😊 | W | 1838 | ,, | ,, | ,, | s |
| 1792 | ,, | ,, | ,, | 𝖚 | 1815 | ,, | ,, | ,, | O | 1839 | ,, | ,, | ,, | t |
| 1793 | ,, | ,, | ,, | 𝖔 | 1816 | ,, | ,, | ,, | T | 1840 | ,, | ,, | 😊 | u |
| 1794 | ,, | ,, | ,, | 𝖒 | 1817 | ,, | ,, | ,, | X | 1841 | ,, | ,, | ,, | v |
| 1795 | ,, | ,, | ,, | 𝖖 | 1818 | ,, | ,, | ,, | I | 1842 | ,, | ,, | ,, | x |
| 1796 | ,, | ,, | ,, | 𝖟 | 1819 | ,, | ,, | ,, | V | 1843 | ,, | ,, | ,, | z |

## SHEFFIELD

| | | | | | | | | | | | |
|---|---|---|---|---|---|---|---|---|---|---|---|
| 1844 | 🦁 | 👑 | 👤 | **A** | 1868 | 🦁 | 👑 | 👤 | **A** | 1892 | 🦁 👑 **Z** |
| 1845 | ,, | ,, | ,, | **B** | 1869 | ,, | ,, | ,, | **B** | | |
| 1846 | ,, | ,, | ,, | **C** | 1870 | ,, | ,, | ,, | **C** | | |
| 1847 | ,, | ,, | ,, | **D** | 1871 | ,, | ,, | ,, | **D** | 1893 | 👑 🦁 **a** |
| 1848 | 🦁 | 👑 | ,, | **E** | 1872 | ,, | ,, | ,, | **E** | 1894 | ,, ,, **b** |
| 1849 | ,, | ,, | ,, | **F** | 1873 | 🦁 | 👑 | 👤 | **F** | 1895 | ,, ,, **c** |
| 1850 | ,, | ,, | ,, | **G** | 1874 | ,, | ,, | ,, | **G** | 1896 | ,, ,, **d** |
| 1851 | ,, | ,, | ,, | **H** | 1875 | ,, | ,, | ,, | **H** | 1897 | ,, ,, **e** |
| 1852 | ,, | ,, | ,, | **I** | 1876 | ,, | ,, | ,, | **J** | 1898 | ,, ,, **f** |
| 1853 | ,, | ,, | ,, | **K** | 1877 | ,, | ,, | ,, | **K** | 1899 | ,, ,, **g** |
| 1854 | ,, | ,, | ,, | **L** | 1878 | ,, | ,, | ,, | **L** | 1900 | ,, ,, **h** |
| 1855 | ,, | ,, | ,, | **M** | 1879 | ,, | ,, | ,, | **M** | 1901 | ,, ,, **i** |
| 1856 | ,, | ,, | ,, | **N** | 1880 | ,, | ,, | ,, | **N** | 1902 | ,, ,, **k** |
| 1857 | ,, | ,, | ,, | **O** | 1881 | ,, | ,, | ,, | **O** | 1903 | ,, ,, **l** |
| 1858 | ,, | ,, | ,, | **P** | 1882 | ,, | ,, | ,, | **P** | 1904 | ,, ,, **m** |
| 1859 | ,, | ,, | ,, | **R** | 1883 | ,, | ,, | ,, | **Q** | 1905 | ,, ,, **n** |
| 1860 | ,, | ,, | ,, | **S** | 1884 | ,, | ,, | ,, | **R** | 1906 | ,, ,, **o** |
| 1861 | ,, | ,, | ,, | **T** | 1885 | ,, | ,, | ,, | **S** | 1907 | ,, ,, **p** |
| 1862 | ,, | ,, | ,, | **U** | 1886 | ,, | ,, | ,, | **T** | 1908 | ,, ,, **q** |
| 1863 | ,, | ,, | ,, | **V** | 1887 | ,, | ,, | ,, | **U** | 1909 | ,, ,, **r** |
| 1864 | ,, | ,, | ,, | **W** | 1888 | ,, | ,, | ,, | **V** | 1910 | ,, ,, **s** |
| 1865 | ,, | ,, | ,, | **X** | 1889 | ,, | ,, | ,, | **W** | 1911 | ,, ,, **t** |
| 1866 | ,, | ,, | ,, | **Y** | 1890 | ,, | ,, | ,, | **X** | 1912 | ,, ,, **u** |
| 1867 | ,, | ,, | ,, | **Z** | 1891 | ,, | ,, | ,, | **Y** | 1913 | ,, ,, **v** |

## SHEFFIELD

| 1914 | 🛡 🦁 | 𝔀 | 1936 | 🛡 🦁 | t | 1958 | 🛡 🦁 | Q |
|---|---|---|---|---|---|---|---|---|
| 1915 | ,, ,, | 𝔵 | 1937 | ,, ,, | u | 1959 | ,, ,, | R |
| 1916 | ,, ,, | 𝔶 | 1938 | ,, ,, | V | 1960 | ,, ,, | S |
| 1917 | ,, ,, | 𝔷 | 1939 | ,, ,, | W | 1961 | ,, ,, | T |
| | | | 1940 | ,, ,, | X | 1962 | ,, ,, | U |
| 1918 | 🛡 🦁 | a | 1941 | ,, ,, | y | 1963 | ,, ,, | V |
| 1919 | ,, ,, | b | 1942 | ,, ,, | Z | 1964 | ,, ,, | W |
| 1920 | ,, ,, | c | | | | 1965 | ,, ,, | X |
| 1921 | ,, ,, | d | 1943 | ,, ,, | A | 1966 | ,, ,, | Y |
| 1922 | ,, ,, | e | 1944 | ,, ,, | B | 1967 | ,, ,, | Z |
| 1923 | ,, ,, | f | 1945 | ,, ,, | C | 1968 | ,, ,, | 𝒜 |
| 1924 | ,, ,, | g | 1946 | ,, ,, | D | 1969 | ,, ,, | ℬ |
| 1925 | ,, ,, | h | 1947 | ,, ,, | E | 1970 | ,, ,, | C |
| 1926 | ,, ,, | i | 1948 | ,, ,, | F | 1971 | ,, ,, | D |
| 1927 | ,, ,, | k | 1949 | ,, ,, | G | 1972 | ,, ,, | ℰ |
| 1928 | ,, ,, | l | 1950 | ,, ,, | H | 1973 | ,, ,, | ℱ |
| 1929 | ,, ,, | m | 1951 | ,, ,, | I | 1974 | ,, ,, | G |
| 1930 | ,, ,, | n | 1952 | 🛡 🦁 👑 | K | 1975 | 🛡 🦁 | 𝒜 |
| 1931 | ,, ,, | o | 1953 | ,, ,, | L | 1976 | ,, ,, | ℬ |
| 1932 | ,, ,, | p | 1954 | ,, ,, | M | 1977 | ,, ,, 👑 | C |
| 1933 | 🛡 🦁 👑 | q | 1955 | ,, ,, | N | 1978 | ,, ,, | D |
| 1934 | ,, ,, | r | 1956 | ,, ,, | O | 1979 | ,, ,, | ℰ |
| 1935 | ,, ,, | s | 1957 | ,, ,, | P | 1980 | ,, ,, | ℱ |
| | | | | | | 1981 | ,, ,, | 𝒢 |

Subsequent date
letters as for London.

## YORK

| | | |
|---|---|---|
| 1700 | | 1807 |
| 1701 " " " | | 1808 " " " " |
| | | similar shields to |
| 1702 " " " | | 1811 " " " " |
| 1703 " " " | | 1812 " " " |
| 1704, 1707, 1709, 1710, 1712, No records available | | 1813 " " " " |
| | | similar shields to |
| 1705 " " " | | 1830 " " " |
| | | similar shields to |
| 1706 " " " | | 1836 " " " " |
| 1708 " " " | | 1837 " " " |
| 1711 " " " | | 1838 " " " " |
| 1713 " " " | | 1839 " " " " |
| Assay office closed 1717 — 1773. No records available 1774 — 1777. | | 1840 " " " |
| | | 1841 " " " " |
| 1778 | | 1842 " " " " |
| 1779 " " " | | 1843 " " " " |
| similar shields to | | 1844 " " " " |
| 1784 " " | | 1845 " " " " |
| 1785 " " " | | similar shields to |
| 1786 " " | | 1848 " " " " |
| 1787 | | 1849 " " " " |
| 1788 " " " | | 1850 |
| 1789 " " " | | 1851 " " " " |
| 1790 " " " | | similar shields to |
| 1791 " " " | | 1856 " " " |
| 1792 " " " " | | |
| similar shields to | | |
| 1805 " " " " | | |
| 1806 " " " " | | |

# Index